Delivering Hope

Delivering Hope: Leading a Business That Builds the Kingdom of God
Todd Stewart

©2025 All Rights Reserved. No portion of this book may be reproduced, stored in a retrieval system, or transmitted in any form or by any means—electronic, mechanical, photocopy, recording, scanning, or other—except for brief quotations in critical reviews or articles without the prior permission of the author.

Editors: Karla Dial and Kristin Spann

Scripture quotations marked ESV are taken from the ESV® Bible (The Holy Bible, English Standard Version®). Copyright © 2001 by Crossway, a publishing ministry of Good News Publishers. All rights reserved.

Scripture quotations marked NASB are taken from the (NASB®) New American Standard Bible®. Copyright © 1960, 1971, 1977, 1995, 2020 by The Lockman Foundation. Used by permission. All rights reserved. www.lockman.org.

Scripture quotations marked NIV are taken from the Holy Bible, New International Version®, NIV®. Copyright © 1973, 1978, 1984, 2011 by Biblica, Inc.® Used by permission of Zondervan. All rights reserved worldwide. www.zondervan.com. The "NIV" and "New International Version" are trademarks registered in the United States Patent and Trademark Office by Biblica, Inc.®

Any internet addresses, phone numbers, or company or product information printed in this book are offered as a resource and are not intended in any way to be or to imply an endorsement by Todd Stewart, nor does Todd Stewart vouch for the existence, content, or services of these sites, phone numbers, companies, or products beyond the life of this book.

Published by Game Changer Publishing

Paperback ISBN: 978-1-969372-17-9
Hardcover ISBN: 978-1-969372-70-4
Digital ISBN: 978-1-969372-19-3

www.GameChangerPublishing.com

Why not choose to run a great business for a greater purpose?

—Todd Stewart

To Jesus, my Savior and King, this labor of love would not be possible apart from your grace and mercy in the life of our family!

"You make known to me the path of life; in your presence there is fullness of joy; at your right hand are pleasures forevermore."
(Psalm 16:11 ESV)

The Stewart Family Legacy
Family Symbol ~ Cross
Vision ~ Every generation faithfully following Jesus
Mission ~ Abide in Christ & live on mission
Values Statement ~ Our values CROSS every divide:
Faith (Hebrews 11:1)
Stewardship (Luke 12:48)
Love (1 Corinthians 13:13)
Unity (Ephesians 4:3)
Mission (Matthew 28:19–20)

Endorsements

"Todd Stewart has lived a life of vibrant stewardship of both business relationships as well as economic opportunities for the building up of the Kingdom of God. This is a refreshing, immensely helpful book about how to manage resources and relationships for the eternal benefit of people in great need, as well as one's colleagues in the workplace!"

—*Ellen Vaughn,* New York Times *bestselling author*

"If you've ever wondered whether your faith belongs at work, this book will settle that issue once and for all. If you don't need convincing, but you haven't been able to figure out how to blend your vocation with your heart for ministry, congratulations. The good news is, you are holding a valuable tutorial. Todd Stewart's words in *Delivering Hope* will not only inspire you to use your business as a mission field for the glory of God, but it will also show you how to begin, right where you are."

—*Shellie Rushing Tomlinson, Bible teacher and author,* Don't Try to Pray Like Her

"Todd and Nikki Stewart are bellows stoking fires of the Holy Spirit, blowing embers of hope in Jesus around the globe. *Delivering Hope* will inspire and challenge you and your business to calibrate around biblical moral values and strategies to succeed in the marketplace and in sharing the gospel, from your neighborhood to the nations."

—*Dave Donaldson, CEO, CityServe International*

"Todd's love for Jesus Christ drives his passion for others to experience the same hope that he's found. His life, as told through the stories in this book, will both inspire and challenge you to think more deeply and intentionally about the alignment of every aspect of your life with the pursuit of God. Eugene Peterson spoke of living a life that is "a long obedience in the same direction." This book is a transparent example of what that looks like in the life of a real person. I am deeply grateful for the years Todd has served on ICM's board and the countless lives he has impacted for Jesus all around the world."

—Janice Rosser Allen, CEO,
Int'l Cooperating Ministries

"As I read Todd's family story, it painted an inspiring picture of marketplace ministry and how God uses normal people everywhere to accomplish the extraordinary. His story tells of a company reborn to embrace shared godly values: stewardship, integrity, service, and excellence. The strong foundation he laid became one of a kingdom legacy unfolding. This story shows his love for everyone around him: his employees, the lost and broken, and those who would cross his path. I have known this family for over a decade, and their story has impacted my family and children—and youth and families all over southern Africa—in a profound manner. My prayer is that this would be just the beginning, that the children of those mentioned in this book will dream dreams even bigger than Todd's generation did, dreams so big they go beyond what we can imagine to see God's kingdom established on Earth as it is in heaven. This inspiring book is well worth the read. Well done, my friend."

—Dr. Jacques van Bommel, CEO and founder,
Reaching a Generation Group

"If you are serious about faith and business, I wholeheartedly recommend this book. Todd's remarkable story shows they can flourish together to powerfully impact the Kingdom of God. I've seen Todd live this out in his company, family, and daily life. He doesn't just offer theory, but practical wisdom from years of intentional leadership in both realms. Todd transformed his company by prioritizing people over profit, establishing God-honoring ethical standards, and creating space for spiritual growth in a competitive marketplace. He emphasizes stewardship—that our businesses, talents, and resources ultimately belong to God. This offers a compelling blueprint for businesses to follow, yielding generational legacy and blessing far beyond the bottom line. This can be your story too."

—*Chris Kouba, Lead Pastor,*
United City Church

"The story of the Stewart family, Todd, and the Gulf Winds business will truly 'deliver hope.' Todd is a trophy of God's grace, and the business is a case study in business-as-ministry. The lessons, adventures, faith decisions, and truth of this will inspire you to ask God for more in your own adventure story! These are real people, a real business, the real deal, and represent real hope, if you're ready."

—*Mike Sharrow, CEO,*
C12 Business Forums

"I've been blessed to have walked the ups and downs of life and business with Todd Stewart. He is the real deal! *Delivering Hope* is a must-read for any business owner who wants to use their platform as a vehicle to positively impact the world!"

—*Jeff Thomas, founder, Arkos Global Advisors;*
host, Generous Business Owner *podcast*

"Todd's life work is so powerfully demonstrated in *Delivering Hope*. He faces the challenges of a legacy company, business negotiations, and the ethical decisions surrounding business, and he handles them brilliantly. It's truly inspiring to see how he weaves his moral character and life lessons into a story we can all benefit from. Kudos, my friend... Well done!!!"

—*Flip Flippen, founder and chairman,*
The Flippen Group

"What you hold in your hand is more than a book... it is a powerful testament of the transformative and redemptive power of God in the life of a broken, humble, and steadfast servant leader that will both challenge and change you by sharing his life's journey. Todd has given us a front-row seat to God's purpose at work in our lives. It is a must read!"

—*Davin Salvagno, author of* Finding Purpose at Work *and* Thieves of Purpose

"The Bible has a lot to say about our work. Forty-five of the fifty-two parables Jesus told had a workplace context; the twelve apostles Jesus called were all basically businessmen; and thirty-nine of the forty miracles recorded in the book of Acts took place in the workplace. *Delivering Hope* does a great job of showing how our work can bring satisfaction to our souls as well as significance to our communities."

—*Doctor Bruce Frank, lead pastor,*
Biltmore Church in Asheville, NC

"*Delivering Hope* is a great 'how to' for business leaders who want to have an eternal impact. It is fun, fast-paced, fascinating, and faith-filled. I highly recommend it!"

—*Janet Ward Black, attorney and founder, Ward Black Law; past president, North Carolina Bar Association; member, C12; board member, ICM*

"This testimony of the Stewart family business gives unique insight into what a Christ-led company/corporation should look like. As believers in Jesus, we surrender our lives to Him but rarely surrender our businesses. Yet, a dynamic, eternal legacy shift takes place from corporate levels to the factory when business CEOs lead by godly example. Thank you, Todd, for this rare insight into how God will exceedingly bless our business, order our steps, direct our path, and enlarge our territories . . . when we put Him first."

—*D.L. Bollinger, certified interior designer and herbalist, teacher, master gardener, and author of* Rabbit Trails Redirect

Read This First

Just to say thanks for buying and reading my book,
I would like to connect with you!

Scan the QR Code Here:

Delivering Hope

Leading a Business That Builds the Kingdom of God

Todd Stewart

Contents

Introduction xv

1. Risking It ALL! 1
2. Finding Identity 7
3. The Identity Crisis 13
4. The Buyout 23
5. Transition from Founder-Led to Mission-Led Organization 29
6. The Value of C12 33
7. The Trials of Life and Leadership 39
8. Take a Trip with God! 49
9. The Bus Ride and Defining Moments 63
10. More Than the Move 71
11. The Importance of Unity 81
12. Playing the Shuffle 89
13. The Four Spiritual Secrets 95
14. Times of Transition 101
15. The Good News! 109
16. Multiplying Ministry Through a Sale 115

    Acknowledgments 127

Introduction
The Harvest Is Plentiful, the Laborers Few

"And Jesus went throughout all the cities and villages, teaching in their synagogues and proclaiming the gospel of the kingdom and healing every disease and every affliction. When he saw the crowds, he had compassion for them, because they were harassed and helpless, like sheep without a shepherd. Then he said to his disciples, 'The harvest is plentiful, but the laborers are few; therefore pray earnestly to the Lord of the harvest to send out laborers into his harvest.'"
—Matthew 9:35–38 (ESV)

My purpose in writing this book is to demonstrate the immense value of faith in the marketplace, to share through real-life testimony how God has used ordinary people in our homegrown logistics business to reach tens of thousands with the transformational love of Jesus Christ.

I will encourage and challenge you by sharing a personal testimony of God using my father's layoff in his fifties to spur the founding of our company. This led us on a faith journey we never saw coming. I will also share some significant personal and business trials that God saw us through, and how faith has directly impacted the mission, vision, and values of our company, which was recently named a top place to work in the USA.

In the Scriptures, God often asked His people to set up memorials in the form of stones, stacked up as a visual testament to current and future generations of His faithful provision and power. Similarly, I am writing this book as a testimony of the *hope* Jesus provides in the workplace, to encourage you to see your business and career as powerful ministry tools that can be used by the grace of God to create catalytic impact in the lives of people!

We live in a world that tells us that faith and business are mutually exclusive, but that has not been our story. In fact, just the opposite is true. We believe that building a great business for a greater purpose creates immense value for our team members, the local community, and the entire world. Billy Graham said, "I believe that one of the next great moves of God is going to be through the believers in the workplace."[1] This bold challenge has played itself out in my career and our company. It is my belief that we are better together, and that God is bringing His followers together through organizations like C12 to meet people in their time of need, proving the timeless value of biblical principles and the Gospel of Jesus Christ.

My hope is that you meet God in these pages and are encouraged to grow in your personal witness, living out your faith in a new and fresh way to the glory of God! There is no greater calling!

---

[1] This quote is attributed to Billy Graham in early 2000, quoted in Trevor Freeze, "Coca-Cola Bottler CEO Talks Purpose, Legacy at the Billy Graham Library's Men's Lunch," *Billy Graham Evangelistic Association*, May 23, 2023, https://billygraham.org/articles/coca-cola-bottler-ceo-talks-purpose-legacy-at-the-billy-graham-librarys-mens-lunch.

Chapter 1
Risking It ALL!

"I am convinced that life is 10 percent what happens to me and 90 percent how I respond."
— Charles R. Swindoll

In the mid-1990s, my father, Steve Stewart, did the unthinkable. After being laid off during a merger between two major steamship lines and with no available business financing, he and my mother cashed in their hard-earned 401(k) savings to start Gulf Winds International—a third-party logistics company in Houston, Texas, dedicated to the warehousing and transportation of international containerized freight.

Over the next twenty-five years, Gulf Winds would become an industry leader and the largest container hauler by volume out of the Port of Houston, with a warehouse footprint of over a million square feet. We did not know at the time that God was taking our family and team members through an incredible journey that would lead many to faith and fund massive ministry efforts locally and around the globe, impacting tens of thousands of people with the Good News of Jesus Christ.

My parents took an enormous leap of faith at the age of fifty-two, especially after banks told Dad he was the wrong color and the wrong sex to gain financing. As an emergency backup, my mom held on to only $4,000. But after Dad realized the job market isn't kind to middle-aged executives, he jumped full-steam ahead into the American free-market dream and built his own company from the ground up. If my mother had not been working as a full-time nurse to help support our family at the time, it probably never would have happened. I recall my mom in tears at times, watching their savings slowly drain. But I agree wholeheartedly with the saying "Behind every great man is a great woman." While Mom has never worked in the business, Gulf Winds would not be here today without her approval and support.

Gulf Winds—about MORE than moving freight!

Brenda & Steve Stewart, Mom and Dad

Delivering Hope

The original Gulf Winds family, beginning a new adventure! (1996)

In April 1996, with a commitment from a single customer, Gulf Winds opened its doors at 3240 South Loop East in Houston, Texas. I was a senior in college at the time, and right after graduating, I joined the company as a laborer and forklift operator. My wage was $250 per week, and Dad did not take a paycheck for himself for the first couple of years. Yet by November 1996, the company was one month away from going broke. Dad and his partner called a luncheon meeting with Mom and told her they needed that final $4,000. Without it, the company would sink.

She was given no reason why, and she didn't ask. Her anxiety at the time felt indescribable. Suddenly, the weight of the world sat on her shoulders. Although she was working full-time, things were tight, and she understood that Dad wouldn't be drawing a salary for at least two years. Even with that, though, the savings might not be enough to save the company. There were no guarantees. But she knew the importance of the business to Dad and our family's future, so she took another leap of faith. Lots of sleepless nights and many tears filled the next few months, but great blessings were to come.

In time, we turned the corner. Today, we have more than 120 team members and more than 500 trucks with terminal locations in Houston, Dallas, and Fort Worth, Texas; Memphis, Tennessee; and Mobile, Alabama.

The Scriptures tell us, *"We can make our plans, but the Lord determines our steps"* (Proverbs 16:9 NLT). Dad never planned to start Gulf Winds. Difficult mid-life circumstances forced him to a decision point, and he chose to take the road less traveled. Nearly thirty years later, I am humbled and challenged by his huge step of faith, as well as his sacrifices and generosity toward those who joined our team early on. Thousands of people have benefited from his difficult decision to risk it all when most would decide to settle or call it quits and consider retirement.

Dad—a bold, self-sacrificing businessman

Dad and I on a trip to Colorado in 2012

Delivering Hope

Mom and Dad modeled sacrificial love

He chose to plant and invest in others instead of becoming bitter about the layoff—and those seeds have produced a hundredfold return. I know I speak for many when I express my gratitude to him and my mom for their sacrifices in that difficult season.

Questions to Consider

1. Has the Gulf Winds story inspired you to look at a situation or decision you may be facing differently? If so, how?
2. What sacrifice can you make today that will lead to a harvest tomorrow?
3. Have you ever considered the reality that your best and most purpose-filled days are still ahead of you?

Chapter 2
Finding Identity

"I have been crucified with Christ. It is no longer I who live, but Christ who lives in me. And the life I now live in the flesh I live by faith in the Son of God, who loved me and gave himself up for me."
—Galatians 2:20 (ESV)

I was seventeen years old when my grandfather, dying of cancer, called me into his hospital room to tell me I needed Jesus Christ in my life. Years later, I found out that my grandfather had not spoken for several days before that. I was the oldest grandchild by eight years, and those were the last words I recall him speaking to me. I had no way of comprehending at the time the immeasurable value of the treasure he laid at my feet that day. Little did I know, his words were seeds of faith that would produce a great harvest in God's time.

I would like to tell you that I went home and immediately started following the Lord, but that was not the case. Like most seventeen-year-old high school seniors, my identity was wrapped up in sports, dating my high school sweetheart, and living it up on the weekends. I went off to college at Stephen F. Austin State University a few months later and eventually joined the Sigma Chi fraternity, where, along with my pledge class, I majored in partying. I considered myself a moral guy who liked to have a good time.

Todd Stewart

In my junior year of college, a friend introduced me to a beautiful girl named Nikki at a sports bar in Nacogdoches, Texas called Sports Shack. She was wearing a red dress, and it was love at first sight. I went home and called my mom at 2:00 in the morning and told her I had found "the one." My mom not only thought I was crazy, but asked if I had been drinking.

On our first date, Nikki presented me with the ultimate identity question. "Are you a Christian?" she asked.

Without hesitation, I said, "Yes, I am a Methodist."

Engagement photo of Nikki and I in the Polk County Enterprise newspaper, 1996.

I had not grown up going to church except at Easter and Christmas—but there was a picture of me as a baby being christened at a Methodist church, so I figured that sealed the deal, and I was good enough for Nikki. We got married on July 12, 1997. But the truth is that I was not a Christian and had zero idea what following Jesus Christ was all about.

After I graduated from college in 1996, I returned to Houston to join Gulf Winds International full-time. Nikki graduated a year later; after the wedding, she joined me in Houston and taught kindergarten at a local elementary school. My professional career and identity were taking shape, and it was a blast!

Two years into the business, a friend from my high school football team, Jamie Polk, invited me to start attending a men's Bible study called *Point Man* by Steve Farrar. Honestly, as a young man in my second year of marriage, I was just in it to figure out a little more about marriage and to play basketball afterward. Little did I know that God was about to rock my world.

Nikki and I started attending church and a small group study at Humble Area First Baptist Church (now United City Church), and I

Delivering Hope

began reading the Bible for the first time in my life. The Bible says, *"All scripture is breathed out by God and profitable for teaching, for reproof, for correction, and for training in righteousness, that the man of God may be complete, equipped for every good work"* (2 Timothy 3:16-17 ESV). In a matter of just a couple of months, God so opened my eyes to the truth and practical application of His Word that I realized this whole Christian thing was actually for real! For the first time in my life, I was beginning to see the immeasurable value and beauty of God.

My first sale, arrived! Gulf Winds loading dock, 1997

I will never forget sitting in the pew one Sunday morning, listening to a pastor preach a message titled, "God Is Going to Give You Opportunities, and You Have to Seize the Moment." I had tears in my eyes! It was like God was speaking directly to me through this man and the Bible. I could no longer be a spectator. It was time to get up out of my seat and respond to God's call.

> *For the first time in my life, I was beginning to see the immeasurable value and beauty of God.*

While I had mouthed the words to ask for forgiveness of my sins in the past, I had never truly made Jesus the Lord of my life. I was dead spiritually in my sin, and only Jesus could tell my heart to beat again. I later learned that the prompting and conviction in my heart and spirit was God's amazing love drawing me to Himself.

I walked forward that day during the time of invitation and was baptized soon after at Humble First Baptist Church. I will never forget the overwhelming sense of thankfulness and peace I experienced after rising from the baptismal waters and hearing the beautiful lyrics of the song playing over the loudspeaker in the sanctuary:

> *White as snow*
> *White as snow*
> *Though my sins were like scarlet,*
> *Lord, I know, Lord, I know*
> *That I am free and forgiven*
> *By the power of the cross*
> *By faith in You, I know that I can be*
> *White as snow*

All I could do was raise my hands and worship the One who had died in my place. I had become a Christian, and my identity was found and rooted in the person and work of Jesus Christ. Before God opened my eyes to the magnitude of His love, they had been closed to spiritual things. I had not been interested in them because I valued the things of this world and my own self-serving desires more than God. I pursued my own desires more often than I care to admit, even knowing that pleasure and the desires of this world only provided temporary satisfaction in the moment.

After God opened my eyes and heart to His love and the powerful truths found in His Word, He became the most beautiful and valuable thing to me in the whole world. I experienced what the Scriptures describe as "the new birth" through a personal relationship with Jesus Christ. I had known about God for some time, but after being born again, I really began to know God personally. The more I studied God's Word and applied it to my life, the more I experienced a newfound peace in my soul that still surpasses my understanding. While I always valued the outdoors, my new birth gave me a heightened sense of God's power and presence in all of creation. As a father and husband, the new birth caused me to see my wife and kids with exponential value, to cherish and nurture them. The new birth caused me to see my job as a ministry opportunity intended to reach other people with the immeasurable love and grace of Jesus Christ! The new birth allows us to find our true purpose in this life and provides a certain hope for our eternal home!

I love the way pastor and author John Piper puts it: "God is most glorified in us, when we are most satisfied in Him."[2] Our true identity is found in God!

Questions to Consider

1. Where do you find your identity?
2. Do you feel more like a spectator or an active player in your faith?
3. What is preventing you from reading the Bible or joining a Bible study group, either in person or online?

---

[2] John Piper, *Desiring God*, rev. ed. (Multonomah, 2011), 5.

Chapter 3

The Identity Crisis

"According to the Pew Research Center, about 40 percent of all workers say their job or career is highly important to their sense of identity."[3]
— Pew Research Center, *How Americans View Their Jobs*

At the end of Gulf Winds' first year of operation, Dad's 401(k) had just about run out. By the grace of God, we managed to get through December 1996, and in January 1997, we turned the corner, started the trucking company, and started to grow our warehousing business. I was spending significant time working inside and outside during this season, doing a little bit of everything as I continued to pitch in wherever needed. With cash running very low, we managed to factor our receivables at a high interest rate for a season and ultimately gain traditional financing options.

Gulf Winds was starting to take off, and I was growing personally, professionally, and spiritually. The vision was taking shape, and I was getting the opportunity to help build things from the ground up. I was president-in-training, and so proud of our little company.

---

[3] Juliana Menasce Horowitz and Kim Parker, *How Americans View Their Jobs: 2023 Report*, Pew Research Center, March 30, 2023, https://news.gallup.com/poll/175400/workers-sense-identity-job.aspx.

Dad and I receiving a Rotary Club Award in 2012

And it seemed my hunger for the Word of God increased by the second. *"As a deer pants for flowing streams, so pants my soul for you, O God"* (Psalm 42:1 ESV). I recall every sermon and Bible study lesson speaking right to my heart during that period. *How could I have been so blind for so long?* I thought. As I began to mature through studying the Scriptures, I understood that what I had been missing were the eyes of faith. Many passages in the Bible speak about those who are blind and deaf to the truth. Before coming to faith, I was *"always learning, but never able to arrive at a knowledge of the truth"* (2 Timothy 3:7 ESV). After, I was applying the first to gain the second.

Jesus explains this mystery in Mark 4 when He says, *"The secret of the kingdom of God has been given to you. But to those on the outside, everything is said in parables so that, 'they may be ever seeing but never perceiving, and ever hearing but never understanding; otherwise they might turn and be forgiven!'"* (NIV). The eyes of faith are a gift that we must receive to have a fruitful relationship with God.

Delivering Hope

"For by grace you have been saved through faith. And this is not your own doing; it is the gift of God, not a result of works, so that no one may boast."
—Ephesians 2:8–9 (ESV)

One Sunday morning, a guest preacher named Bobby Welch from Daytona Beach, Florida, spoke to our congregation on Jeremiah 8:20, which reads, *"The harvest has passed, the summer is ended, and we are not saved"* (ESV). This message hit me so deeply that I recall tearfully buying a cassette tape of the sermon afterward. In those days, we did not have access to sermons online. My heart was starting to break for what breaks God's heart—and nothing hurts His heart more than people who are lost and hurting, who do not know Jesus Christ as Lord and Savior. I wanted to tell others about Jesus, but honestly had no idea where to start. I had not grown up in church, so I felt ill-equipped to share the Good News that had begun to transform my heart and soul.

Thankfully, our senior pastor at the time, Dr. Bruce Frank, decided to lead our entire church in FAITH evangelism training. (FAITH stands for Forsaking All I Trust Him.) Hundreds of churches across the country were conducting this training at the time. I signed up immediately, excited to join a team that would go out in our community to share the Good News. I was also fearful and nervous, since I was just a baby Christian and concerned I would not know what to say or how to respond to questions about faith and the Bible. But my team leader turned out to be our senior pastor, Dr. Bruce Frank! This was wonderful, because I had the best teacher I could possibly have. But it also was terrifying, because I did not want to disappoint him—or worse, embarrass myself and our team with my lack of biblical knowledge.

Pastor Bruce taught us all how to share the Gospel with the FAITH tool. I will never forget the day we pulled into a driveway a few weeks into training, and he turned to me and said, "You see that door? That one is yours." As my anxiety level shot sky-high, we all prayed.

Afterward, I shared the FAITH outline with the people we were visiting, and most importantly, my personal faith story.

To my surprise, many of the people we visited during that time responded positively to my testimony—and more importantly, to the Gospel. I was elated, as was our team, and we continued to go out together on Sunday evenings for a few months. We saw many people confess their sins, surrender their lives to Jesus, and receive the immeasurable gift of salvation during that season.

Shortly thereafter, I volunteered to become a FAITH team leader. I was amazed at the results we had been seeing. I didn't have to be a pastor or long-time Christian to share my faith! I just had to be obedient to God's call on my life and trust that He would do His part to open their eyes and ears to the truth. While I didn't realize it at the time, God clearly was cultivating the gift of evangelism in my spirit.

I recall walking door-to-door one Sunday evening with a guy I practically had to drag along with me. He really did not want to be there but knew he should participate, since God calls us to share the Good News with others. The first door we knocked on was answered by a guy who had been drinking heavily, judging by his breath. He turned out to be one of the rare ones who rejected us right out of the gate. After that, my friend lagged behind, not wanting to go to the next house. I left him at the curb and continued on. To my delight, the inebriated man's next-door neighbor invited me in, so I quickly motioned to my buddy to join me. Half embarrassed, he sprinted up to the porch, and we then sat at the dining room table with the older gentleman. To our delight, after a few minutes of sharing, our newfound friend confessed his sins and prayed to receive Jesus Christ as Lord and Savior on the spot!

As we left, my teammate just hung his head. He said, "That felt like a gut punch from the Lord." I encouraged him, and we celebrated God's saving work in the life of our new friend and brother in Christ with the church when we returned from our visits that evening.

It's not our job to save people, but we are called to plant seeds

Delivering Hope

through sharing our testimony and the Gospel. The Lord does the rest in His time. Sometimes it happens on the spot, and other times it may take years of planting and watering seeds before any root of faith takes hold.

To my joy and my mom's delight, Dad began noticing my upbeat attitude when Nikki and I joined them for dinner on Sunday evenings. My father started to show an interest in Christianity, and shortly thereafter, he started taking my mom to a little church down the street from their house.

My dad went on to trust Christ soon after, around the age of fifty-seven, and was baptized. During a conversation about the Gospel, Dad told his pastor he hoped it was not too late for him. The pastor assured him that it is never too late to trust the Lord, as long as a person is breathing.

God transformed my dad's life! I love the testimony he and my mom shared a few years later: They said, "Our marriage is better in our sixties than it was in our thirties because of Jesus." It is so wonderful that God reaches people of all ages with His mercy and grace.

I recall a long-time business associate of my father's who was struggling with addiction and confided in him. He said, "Steve, how did you do it?"

Dad simply responded, "I did not do it—Jesus healed me." We don't know why some come to faith early and others later in life, but the joy is the same, and Heaven is the destination for both!

God moved in my heart so much during this season of faith that I started to look for opportunities to share during the week as well as on Sundays. One Monday morning, I was giving one of our employees a ride to work because his truck had broken down. I decided to go for it and share the Lord with him as we drove over the Ship Channel Bridge. *He can't jump out while the car is moving, so I should be okay*, I thought. I planted the Gospel seed in this man's life, and while he did not jump into a relationship with Christ immediately, he didn't jump out of the car either. This started a friendship and working partnership that has now spanned more than twenty years, and which ultimately resulted in God opening his heart with the gift of faith.

Just as I had experienced with my grandfather when I was seventeen, not all seeds take root immediately. I had to learn this lesson over time. I desperately wanted everyone to experience the joy and forgiveness that I knew. God presented me with countless opportunities to share the Gospel at work, and I count each one a true blessing. Many days, I found myself worshiping the Lord with tears of joy in my truck during my commute, thanking God for every opportunity. It is so exciting to see God move in a person's life and remove the weight of sin and shame. Truly, there is no greater joy than to know that someone has released their sin and embraced the joy found in the Good News of Jesus Christ.

During that season, God really began to stir my heart by giving me opportunities to teach and share the Gospel. Up to that point, my greatest love and purpose aside from my family had been my work, but that shifted rapidly as God poured out His overwhelming love on me. Nothing compares to His everlasting love and kindness. He is all-consuming. My priorities became God, family, and then work. There were many days during that period when I really struggled to understand and find my true purpose. There I was, an only child, president-in-training for a growing and reputable business, yet the Gospel of Jesus Christ continually pulled me. I later learned that I was struggling with a call to full-time pastoral ministry.

> *My greatest love and purpose aside from my family had been my work, but that shifted rapidly as God poured out His overwhelming love on me.*

The calling never let up as work continued, so I decided to take a few classes at Southwestern Baptist Theological Seminary. I loved it and did well in the classes, and I continued to make the most of opportunities to share the Gospel with those in need at work.

Delivering Hope

One of the memories of those people that has stuck with me was a warehouse operator named Jimmy Gonzalez, whom I had known since I was a teenager. In high school, I had worked in the summer as a warehouse laborer, where Jimmy served as the lead forklift operator. Jimmy was from a tough family and a tough neighborhood. He always wore a red bandanna and sported tattoos from head to toe. We could not have been more opposite, yet God was about to bring our worlds back together in a miraculous way.

Our church's interim pastor challenged us to think of one person in our circle of influence who needed to know Jesus, and to pray for that person. He handed each of us in the congregation a red ribbon, representing the saving blood of Jesus Christ, as a reminder to pray for our person. I tied my red ribbon on the door handle of my Dodge pickup truck to remind me to pray for Jimmy each time I got in and out of my vehicle.

I had been doing that for some time when I got a call from our human resources manager saying that Jimmy wanted to talk with me. I saw this as answered prayer. Jimmy came into my office and unloaded some significant personal struggles. Clearly, God had put Jimmy on my heart for a reason. I asked him if he minded if I shared my faith with him, since it had helped me so much in my own life. With a humble heart and tears in his eyes, Jimmy said yes to Jesus that day and has had a true peace about him from that moment on.

We met off and on over the years to discuss Scripture and pray. He would always acknowledge that God's Word seemed to be exactly the message he needed at that moment in time. I had the joy of baptizing Jimmy and his wife at our church.

Jimmy left Gulf Winds a couple of years later, but we stayed in touch. I knew he had been battling some health issues, but I had no idea to what extent. One day, Jimmy's wife, Elisa, came to our office, and I immediately met her in the lobby with a hug. She said she and Jimmy were in town to get cancer treatment, and Jimmy wanted to stop by and see me; he was outside in their car.

I had the honor of baptizing Jimmy's wife, Elisa.

As I walked into the parking lot, I knew in my spirit it would be a difficult visit. The moment I saw Jimmy, I immediately felt the gravity of the situation.

Jimmy had lost about 50 percent of his body weight. He told me he was dying of stomach cancer and asked me to speak at his funeral. I said, "Yes, it would be an honor," and asked if I could pray for him on the spot. We held hands and prayed. His face lit up with a big smile after the prayer; he acknowledged the peace he felt.

A month later, I preached at Jimmy's funeral and shared how God had miraculously worked in his life. Many people were impacted and encouraged by the certainty of Jimmy's new home address in Heaven. Clearly, God was showing me there was much more purpose to working with people in the marketplace than I had considered in the past.

On another occasion, I had to make a sales call on a long-time customer in the Dallas area. This man was a friend, but he was a tough

Delivering Hope

customer, very demanding. We had a good visit concerning service levels and the business in general. But to my surprise, before I left, he handed me a book written by an atheist named Sam Harris, titled *The End of Faith*. Honestly, I was shocked because clearly I was excited about my Christianity, and I believe he knew that at the time. I read some of the book, and we exchanged notes on it.

I decided to return the favor by giving him a book by a converted atheist named Josh McDowell called *More Than a Carpenter*, which my customer read as well. A few days later, he sent me an email noting how the book had moved him about the person and work of Jesus.

I responded by asking if he would be interested in reading a more in-depth version of *More than a Carpenter*. He was very interested, so I sent him a copy of Lee Strobel's wonderful work, *The Case for Christ*. Once again, he devoured it, and shortly afterward, requested an in-person meeting. A couple weeks later, I sat with my tough customer in a little Italian restaurant in Dallas as he wept and received the gift of faith!

But God, who often does abundantly more than we could ever hope or imagine, didn't stop there. In researching churches for my new brother to attend, I came across an amazing teacher named Chuck Swindoll in the Frisco area—the very town where my friend lived, and only a few blocks away from his house! My friend was baptized shortly thereafter in Chuck Swindoll's church. You can't make this stuff up! God is amazing! He pursues us even when we are not interested in Him. He really does leave the ninety-nine to go after the one, as Luke 15 tells us.

There are many more stories I could detail here, but my purpose in sharing these is to show you how God broke my heart for the marketplace. God is fulfilling my desire to be in full-time ministry, but He's doing it in the marketplace, where I get to interact with countless lost people to whom God desires to express His love and grace. My calling to this point in life has been to pastor businesspeople—and it's incredibly exciting to have the opportunity to serve so many people personally, professionally, and spiritually.

"All authority in heaven and on earth has been given to me. Go therefore and make disciples of all nations, baptizing them in the name of the Father and the Son and of the Holy Spirit, teaching them to observe all that I have commanded you. And behold, I am with you always, to the end of the age."
—Matthew 28:18–20 (ESV)

Questions to Consider

1. What is your calling in life?
2. Has my personal faith story challenged you to view your role in the marketplace differently?
3. With whom has God called you to share your story?

Chapter 4
The Buyout

"For what does it profit a man to gain the whole world, and forfeit his soul?"
— Mark 8:36 (ESV)

By the grace of God and with a talented young team of people from varied backgrounds, Gulf Winds quickly became a philanthropic top-tier third-party logistics provider in Houston and Dallas by 2012. Both our warehouse and container-hauling business units experienced significant growth and profitability. Spiritually, we had seen a good number of people come to faith within the business, we had a weekly Bible study, and we were annually giving over six figures to support life-changing nonprofit work in the community and to plant churches around the world.

Before long, we were approaching the elusive $100 million revenue mark, which is very significant for a private company. My father and his partner were by then nearly seventy years old, but our support team (myself included) was all in our late twenties to early forties. We were set for years to come, barring any unforeseen catastrophes, and my father and his partner were able to work when they wanted to and enjoy some of the fruits of their labor the rest of the time.

It was an ideal situation for owners—until various life circumstances in 2014 led to my father's partner asking us to contact an investment banker to "see what the company was worth."

When he started Gulf Winds, my father took on a partner to manage business operations and made him an incredibly generous gift of 50 percent ownership in the business, even though the partner had made no financial investment. That gracious gift was now a huge sticking point, given the immense value of the now-successful business. Ideally, one partner has controlling interest in the business and can make these types of decisions without a deadlock. Unfortunately, we were locked into a 50/50 deal, so any path forward was going to be challenging if our partner was not on the same page.

Honestly, at the time, we had no idea what that short conversation about the value of the company would lead to over the next few years. We went through an extensive show-and-tell process with multiple private equity firms. The more I submitted to it, the more unsettled I became. Nonetheless, our company, employees, strategic warehouse locations, and proprietary container tracking system showed very well, and business was good.

Ocean container tracking has changed the logistics business by allowing importers and exporters to follow their shipments from origin to destination (think about the way you can track your Amazon or FedEx package, but on a global scale). Our ability to collect and consolidate the container location data from multiple steamship lines, railroads, and seaports helped us differentiate ourselves from other transportation providers—especially with high-volume importers that were looking for ways to keep tabs on their ocean shipment inventory. While the data was available to everyone, it was difficult to collect, consolidate, and present in a meaningful way on a large scale. We found a way to do it, and it resulted in new business and growth opportunities that private equity firms saw as very attractive, a valuable asset.

The private equity firms loved the fact that our team was young, talented, and energized. Even more exciting to them was the reality that even throughout the due diligence process, we were growing—adding new clients nearly every week. "Growth and profitability" is the name of

Delivering Hope

the game in the private equity world.

During that time, we also had the opportunity to share our faith with many people who were interested in checking out the company. I was tasked with playing show-and-tell on bus rides all over town with various private equity firms interested in learning more about Gulf Winds. Those rides consisted of viewing our facilities and telling our story, so I could sprinkle in testimony of how God's hand had helped and guided us along our journey. Many of the private equity managers wanted a boxed-up pattern and plan for Gulf Winds; I always enjoyed leading them to the God story instead.

One of my favorite stories involved our strategic warehouse locations at the Barbours Cut container terminal. Our two 178,000-square-foot facilities are located directly across the street from where the longshoremen unload containers from the ships at the Port of Houston. People always asked how we obtained those locations when they visited. While I would like to say we planned it, that was simply not the case.

> *Many of the private equity managers wanted a boxed-up pattern and plan for Gulf Winds; I always enjoyed leading them to the God story instead.*

The property these buildings sit on had lain undeveloped for many years because of local ordinances in Morgan's Point, Texas. Those who lived on the bay side of the ship channel in Morgan's Point were traditionally well-off financially, and they had managed to prevent the development of this approximately twenty-acre tract of land that served as a noise buffer between the dock and their homes. People had given up on developing the property for commercial use until a gentleman in his eighties who owned and operated a small development company managed to talk the Morgan's Point City Council into letting him build, lease, and sell warehouse facilities there, providing tax revenue to the city.

Someone at the port told him Gulf Winds would be a great potential client, given our various warehouse locations in town and the fact that 99 percent of the cargo we handled included import containers moving through the Barbours Cut Terminal. We were not in a financial position to take on a lease, but the development company took a chance on us—and a few years later, constructed the second building. Initially, the landlord wanted to lease it to someone else, but, once again, took a chance on us after we convinced him of the downside to putting a competitor next door. While we knew we wanted to be close to the port for logistical reasons, we never dreamed we would have the opportunity to operate on land formerly prohibited from development, literally directly across the street from the terminal. We had a talented team and a plan, but this opportunity was a gift from God.

God's abundance on display: more than we could ever ask or imagine!

"The heart of man plans his ways, but the Lord establishes his steps."
—Proverbs 16:9 (ESV)

We did, on rare occasions, get private equity managers on board our company tour bus who were persons of faith, and I could see their eyes light up when we spoke of God's provisional hand of blessing on the business.

Our investment banker managed the bidding process for us, and ultimately, we received a significant and eye-popping offer for the business. As the due diligence process continued, I could sense that any potential buyer would have an impact on our culture, and that was a major concern. My parents and I had significant heartburn over the whole process. What had started out as a what-if scenario was quickly becoming more serious and creating division between my dad and his partner.

I could not come to grips with releasing the business at a time when God was clearly using us to reach countless people with the Good News and support His work locally and around the globe. Both we and our employees maintained many personal friendships throughout the company, and I knew that quite a few people had joined Gulf Winds because of our focus on business as ministry. We were at a major crossroads.

By the end of the process, we were all exhausted, but God was about to do the unthinkable.

After much agonizing, I decided that, given the 50/50 ownership split, we had almost no choice but to go through with the sale and deal with the consequences. We began to pray fervently that God would somehow intervene.

Approximately thirty days before closing, God answered our prayer. Our partner walked into my office, sat down, and proceeded to tell me that he did not think we should go through with the sale. Honestly, to this day, I am not certain why or how he came to that conclusion. I have learned over the years that only God truly knows the motives and intentions of our hearts. No matter the reason, it lifted a huge weight off my shoulders, and I viewed it as a gift from the Lord. I later learned that the private equity firm we were working with had never in its history had a company back out that close to a large payout.

Dad and I viewed this as a "Red Sea moment" for our company: God delivered us from a situation that many people said was impossible. In a 50/50 ownership split, a sale can be forced in a court of law if the partners don't agree. But *"what is impossible with man is possible with God"* (Luke 18:27 ESV). He made a way where there appeared to be no way, and in the coming weeks and months, He would do it again as we worked with a mediator to negotiate an extended-term personal buyout with our partner.

Questions to Consider

1. Do you consider your business to be a ministry? Why or why not?
2. Have you fervently prayed and waited on God in what appears to be an impossible situation in your life or business? If so, what did that look like?
3. Have you ever considered selling your business? If so, how has our story challenged you?

Chapter 5
Transition from Founder-Led to Mission-Led Organization

"Then Moses summoned Joshua and said to him in the presence of all Israel, 'Be strong and courageous, for you must go with this people into the land that the Lord swore to their ancestors to give them, and you must divide it among them as their inheritance. The Lord himself goes before you and will be with you; he will never leave you nor forsake you. Do not be afraid; do not be discouraged.'"
—Deuteronomy 31:7–8 (NIV)

I took over Gulf Winds as president in 2012, just a couple of years before the near-buyout described in Chapter 4. I will never forget my dad telling me that he wanted me to have his corner office by the entryway, and that he would move into my smaller office down the hall. It was a wonderful example of humility on his part, as well as an active endorsement of me in my new role. What a great example for me and others to follow!

So there I was, president of Gulf Winds International, at the age of thirty-five. I had been president-in-training since joining the company at twenty-two, so the transition felt natural but strange at the same time. I did feel a little bit like Joshua taking over from Moses, given my dad's long tenure in the industry and well-recognized name and character. But my support team was very strong, and with a few personnel moves, I felt that our leadership was in good hands.

I knew, though, that Gulf Winds needed clarity concerning our mission, vision, and values. Like most small companies, we had never spent time defining these very important guideposts, so that became my top priority. After much prayer and thought, I enlisted the help of a few people on our executive team as well as a trusted consultant to help with this task. After half a day of off-site deliberation, we had a good draft, and I received clarity on it shortly thereafter. The time was at hand for us to be bold about our intent to glorify God in the business and clearly articulate our identity, purpose, and future as a company.

I was very excited and nervous at the same time. I called the leaders of the company together a few days later and presented them with the mission statement as a filter and guide for all company decisions. I knew some of our people would think I was crazy, but I pressed forward—and that was the best decision I ever could have made as the company's new leader. The statement read:

> *Our mission is to glorify God by providing world-class logistics services through continual investment in our people, our clients, our community, and the world we live in.*
>
> *Our vision is to be the premier third-party logistics provider in the markets we serve.*
>
> *Our values: Faith, Integrity, Stewardship, Service, and Excellence* (Later, we added Humility and Compassion.)

During a recent corporate office move, I discovered an email I had written to my dad and his partner in 2007 during the season when God started leading me toward the true mission and purpose for Gulf Winds—about five years before I became president. It is wonderful to look back now and see that God's plans were in the works long before the buyout even played out:

07/05/2007 08:52 AM

Our values and objectives drive everything about our organization. They tell our employees and customers who we are and how we intend to conduct ourselves personally and professionally. That being said, we need to nail them down and continue to infuse them into our organization. I wrote the following while on the plane back from Richmond to get us started. Please review and let me know what you think. We can build around these company objectives.

Give ALL (100%) of the glory to Jesus Christ for the success of our company.

Project a God-sized vision for the company and operate in faith by believing in what we hope for and being certain of what we cannot see.

Conduct ourselves in a humble manner by removing EGOS and personal agendas, ensuring company-wide success, and minimizing conflict.

Give back to the communities we operate in, recognizing and believing that it is better to give than to receive.

Invest in the ongoing development of our people from a spiritual, academic, and physical perspective, ensuring each person's God-given talents and capabilities are maximized.

Function as a family that properly and fairly rewards and disciplines based on positive and negative results.

Provide growth opportunities for employees who display a commitment to the company and our customers.

Best Regards,
Todd

God took me on the adventure of a lifetime as president of Gulf Winds.

The mission, vision, and values set the tone for the culture. While establishing these guideposts is an essential part of laying a foundation for business as ministry, the more difficult part is ensuring that the people working in the company support and live out these ideals.

Questions to Consider

1. Is your company founder-led or mission-led?
2. Does your company have a clear and God-centered mission, vision, and values statement?
3. How does my father's act of humility challenge you as a servant leader?

Chapter 6
The Value of C12

"Two are better than one; because they have a good return for their labor. For if either of them falls, the one will lift up his companion. But woe to the one who falls when there is not another to lift him up! Furthermore, if two lie down together they keep warm, but how can one be warm alone? And if one can overpower him who is alone, two can resist him. A cord of three strands is not quickly torn apart."
—Ecclesiastes 4:9–12 (NASB)

As many experts have written, leadership is lonely. Thankfully, God intervened in this area for me very early in my new role as president of Gulf Winds. I was serving on the board of a wonderful Virginia-based Christian nonprofit, International Cooperating Ministries, when an older and very wise board member, Ralph Miller, pulled me aside and asked if I had ever heard of a monthly roundtable meeting of Christian CEOs called C12. I had not, but Ralph told me that C12 was launching a chapter in Houston and said I should check it out. He had been a chairperson for many years, so he was speaking from firsthand experience.

My schedule at the time was quite busy, so instead of checking it out personally, I did the next best thing: I called a devoted Christian friend, Simon Lee, who owns the Buy on Purpose office supply company, and asked him to check it out if he had time. Simon is a straight-shooting truth-teller and deeply in love with Jesus. I trust his heart and counsel because I know his goal is to walk in obedience to the Lord and glorify God in every area of His life.

A month later, Simon called and told me that I had to get over to C12 to join the roundtable. Simon raved about the curriculum that was bridging the divide between business and ministry. Most importantly, he spoke about the relationships he was forming with other Christian business owners and told me I would love and connect with the group. It seemed to be a perfect fit to help me accomplish my goal of using business as ministry.

Ralph Miller, a board member of International Cooperating Ministries (ICM), first introduced me to C12. (2019)

After my first C12 meeting, I was hooked. Its mission is to operate great businesses for a greater purpose—the same as mine. I found that my personal testimony and experiences, or growing pains, could help others, and that others had wisdom to share with me as well. Seven other CEOs and I started that first meeting with prayer, and then the leader pulled out a very helpful personal balance–wheel exercise to see how we were doing with marriage and family, discipling others, personal finances, fitness and nutrition, rest and retreat, biblical community, fun and recreation, and most importantly our walk with God. We went through a short devotional that encouraged us all, and a helpful business segment that tied it all together. We were able to share personal and work-related prayer requests and connect at a deeper level with people experiencing similar challenges and pressures.

Delivering Hope

Simon Lee, Jeff Thomas, and I at Taiwan's first C12 CEO interest meeting in Taipei, Taiwan, 2024

One breakthrough that I recall from an early meeting was a member who openly shared his addiction to Dr. Pepper—he was concerned about his health. It seems like a small thing, but he was drinking twelve cans a day, and his health was declining because of it. As he was sharing, my friend, Simon, said he had a word from the Lord for this gentleman. The word was "No more Dr. Pepper." It sounds simple and easy, but if you have ever had an addiction, you can imagine how hard it would be to stop that habit cold turkey! But with God's help and a time of prayer on the spot, that man quit Dr. Pepper that day, and within a few months was in the best shape of his life! That was ten years ago, and to this day, he has not gone back to it.

I saw the power of peer group accountability on display, and I loved it. How awesome that a group of Christian CEOs was meeting monthly to talk about business as ministry! How amazing that we could share personal and professional struggles and get godly counsel in return. I was so taken with C12 that I quickly started contacting other CEOs who

I knew might be interested in joining. I prayed for opportunities to share what God was doing in the group and for Him to bring others to the table. And God delivered more than once.

Our passion at C12, the glory of God!

One transformation story of a friend I ran into at a charity golf tournament sticks with me to this day. I was in my cart preparing to head over to the clubhouse when I saw Brad Maxey, third-generation president of Danner's Incorporated—a seventy-five-year-old family business operating in the maritime and security field. Brad and I had known each other for a long time, as our parents were friends and served on a couple of charitable boards together.

God put Brad on my heart that day concerning C12. I wanted to invite him, but wondered how to approach him because I was not sure where he stood spiritually. Following the prompting of the Holy Spirit, I drove my golf cart over to Brad and greeted him. We spoke for a few minutes; like me, he also had recently taken over for his dad as president of his company. To my delight, the first thing he asked me was, "You

Delivering Hope

don't know of any good coaching groups for CEOs, do you?" *You can't make this stuff up!* I thought, and proceeded to tell him all about my experience with C12. Clearly, this was a divine appointment!

Brad attended his first C12 meeting shortly thereafter, where he opened up about some personal health issues his family was facing. One of our board members felt led to pray for him, and our entire group surrounded him and prayed over him. Brad will tell you now that Christ found him that day, and it has been a joy to watch him grow and see how God has walked with him through the ups and downs of life and ministry since that time. There is a difference in knowing about God and knowing God, as Brad would tell you.

My wife and I ran into Brad at a gala a couple of months after his conversion. As we were leaving, he ran up to us, pulled me aside, and with a bright smile that reflected the Holy Spirit, said, "Man, there is a whole world out there that I never knew existed!" Knowing God makes all the difference!

Today, C12 has more than half a dozen groups meeting in different parts of Houston, and we can't seem to add new chairpersons fast enough to keep up with the expansion. It is truly an exciting time! C12 is not only growing in Texas, but nationally and all around the globe. My friend, Simon, sold his company and moved halfway around the world to launch and grow C12 Taiwan! It's growing like wildfire to the glory of God! I am excited to see how God will continue to use it to impact CEOs and their key employees with best-in-class business-as-ministry curricula and the Good News of Jesus.

I consider it a key mission in life to introduce others to the C12 gift that Ralph Miller presented to me. The intimate prayer and support structure for Christian leaders who are on the front lines of ministry at home, church—and most importantly in the marketplace—is invaluable. As you will see in the next chapter, having a great support structure and firm foundation in Christ is necessary, given all the challenges we face in those three realms.

Steve and Carolyn Van Ootegen (C12 Houston co-chairs), recognizing Simon Lee and I as founding members with ten years' service

Questions to Consider

1. Do you or anyone you know need to connect with a C12 group in your area?
2. Who has God placed on your heart that needs to hear about C12?
3. Do you need God's help to overcome a destructive addiction in your life?
4. How does my story about God prompting me to pursue Brad challenge you? How does Brad's testimony challenge you?

Chapter 7
The Trials of Life and Leadership

"Consider it pure joy, my brothers and sisters, whenever you face trials of many kinds, because you know that the testing of your faith produces perseverance. Let perseverance finish its work, so that you may be mature and complete, not lacking anything."

—James 1:2–4 (NIV)

About a year after I transitioned into the role of president at Gulf Winds, Dad had routine bloodwork at his annual physical that came back abnormal. Dad had always been very healthy and looked about ten years younger than he was at all times. He took great pleasure in our clients thinking we were brothers!

I accompanied him and my mom to the doctor's office to get the results of his bloodwork. I remember him telling Mom, "You know we are not going in here to get good results." He knew that something must have been off, or the doctor would not have called them in for an in-person follow-up.

The doctor walked into the room and put a piece of paper on the table in front of us, which basically outlined the average life span for a person suffering from a blood disease called myelodysplastic syndrome (MDS)—a precursor to acute myeloid leukemia, a serious form of cancer. This was the meeting we all pretend we will never have in this life—the one when the doctor tells us how long we are projected to live.

I recall trying to lighten things up a bit by saying, "Well, we all have a timetable—we just don't have it laid in front of us daily." We prayed, and Dad accepted the news well. Mom struggled much more, since she is a nurse by trade. She also was realizing that her dreams of travel and retirement with Dad, with me in charge of the business, were slipping away.

Life went on as usual for a few months, with Dad being monitored. Eventually, however, he began suffering from shortness of breath. At that point, he started an experimental program, and we all started down a very difficult road, watching him endure the agonizing realities of the treatment regimen and physical challenges that blood cancer brings. Not only were we adjusting to Dad's new normal, but the stressful company buyout episode was playing out in the background during this time, which also took a great toll on all of us.

We cried, the angels rejoiced, and Dad passed on to glory on January 26, 2017. As an only child, I felt the full weight and responsibility for the family, my mom, and the business settling around my shoulders. Fortunately, several people from my leadership team, church, and C12 were praying for me and encouraging me. One of the greatest honors of my life was preaching at my father's funeral and having the opportunity to share the Gospel with countless industry executives, friends, and family members. It was one of the hardest yet most rewarding things I have ever done. There is no greater opportunity to reach people with the Gospel than in these moments of transition from the physical to the eternal.

From a business and ministry perspective, getting through the buyout was freeing—yet at the same time, it carried the weight of fulfilling our obligation to our previous partner. At the tail end of the process, the oil market crashed, and we found ourselves in the challenging position of trying to salvage what had previously been a real

Delivering Hope

boom for our company. We took on significant increases in labor costs during that season, and it was a challenge to keep moving forward with warehouse revenue dropping off substantially.

Things were getting harder, not easier, for me and our leadership team. I was quickly starting to feel more like Moses instead of Joshua. Moses led the people in a time of testing and wandering in the desert. God was very faithful to provide for His people there through miraculous means, but it was a hard time, and God kept them there until they aligned their hearts with His.

In a similar way, my time as president from 2012 to 2020 was filled with many personal, professional, and spiritual challenges. My main concern and prayer for my team was that they would learn to put God first and thereby align their hearts with His. This eventually happened, but it took a lot longer than expected, and we all matured during this time as we were constantly tested with trials of various kinds.

A few of those trials during that season concerned a former employee who sued our company for a significant sum. Also, our house flooded with over 4 feet of water during Hurricane Harvey, my mother-in-law was diagnosed with breast cancer, I found out that a long-time employee had embezzled more than a million dollars from Gulf Winds, and COVID-19 hit. But the most difficult trial we faced during this season concerned our teenage daughter, Lexi Grace Stewart.

Our home post–Hurricane Harvey, 2017; The floods devastated our home both outside and in.

Lexi walked through a significant season of anxiety and depression that was associated with childhood trauma that Nikki and I had never known about; it was a dark time. We raised Lexi with a strong focus on the Lord and had taken her on mission trips from the time she was little. God was always important to Lexi, and I baptized her when she was seven because she would not take no for an answer any longer. When we went on family mission trips, it was not uncommon for her to stand up before adults to share and encourage them, including showing off her gymnastics skills. Lexi was an excellent athlete and successful in all she did, receiving multiple awards in volleyball and track and field. As a gymnast and cheerleader, she ran with the popular crowd at school; there was never a shortage of boys waiting in the wings to date her.

Lexi was a leader in everything she did, so it was very disturbing to me and Nikki when she started to withdraw and hang around a different crowd that had many concerning issues. She started sleeping a lot, and her grades dropped. Nikki was a true warrior during that period; she knew something was way off, and we had to do something to help our daughter.

In December 2018, during the Christmas school break, Nikki reached her breaking point. She asked me to take Lexi to Haiti on a mission trip to serve with My Life Speaks—a wonderful ministry that provides community-enrichment services such as feeding programs and education in a small village.

Our family had traveled there many times, and we considered it a happy place for all of us. Lexi had always connected with many of the special-needs children served by My Life Speaks, so our hope was that God would recenter her heart and

Mission trips to Haiti are always a happy time for our family. (2015)

perhaps she would open up to us about what was going on in her life. I had already been considering the trip, but when Nikki approached me about it—asking me to arrange it for the next day—it was clear it would not be optional for Lexi.

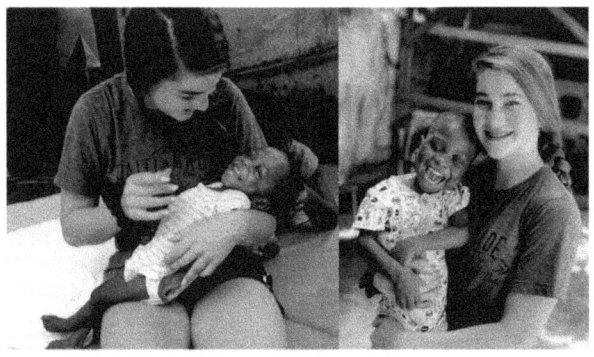

The joy of being loved! (Haiti, 2017)

So I bought two tickets and Lexi got on the plane with me the next day, despite her mixed feelings. I put out an SOS to all of my close friends to pray fervently for us during our time away. We needed a breakthrough desperately!

After our first day in Haiti, I called Lexi over and we sat on a blue concrete bench inside the My Life Speaks compound. My heart was broken for her, and I was asking God to please work a miracle in that moment. After a brief talk, I asked Lexi what was going on and if something had happened to her that we were not aware of. In tears, she finally told me that she had been abused for three years by someone we trusted when she was between the ages of five and seven.

God can do profound works anywhere! (Haiti, 2019)

I was brokenhearted and furious at the same time. We never imagined that such a thing could happen to our family! But it had—and now that the truth was exposed, we could begin to focus on how to help our daughter.

God put three young ladies on that trip who were in their early twenties—Rachel, Anna, and Eden—who helped me not only pray for Lexi in private, but also love her well and speak truth into her life. I spent time in my bunk at night praying fervently the words of Psalm 1 over Lexi's life: *"Blessed is Lexi who walks not in the counsel of the wicked, nor stands in the way of sinners, nor sits in the seat of scoffers; but Lexi's delight is in the law of the Lord, and on his law she meditates day and night. Lexi is like a tree planted by streams of water that yields its fruit in its season and its leaf does not wither. In all that Lexi does, she prospers."*

Lexi and I at a beach in Haiti, then with friends at the My Life Speaks compound

An adult on the trip pulled me aside and shared with me that their son had survived abuse as well. I am amazed by the way God places the right people around us in our time of need when we are seeking Him. Still, the hard work of healing would play out for all three of us over the next couple of years.

Clearly, I was feeling the weight and challenge of leading with a strong Christian purpose and mission. To top it off, Gulf Winds experienced significant increases in labor and insurance rates during

Delivering Hope

that period, making it increasingly more difficult to maintain an acceptable level of profitability, and our revenue grew stagnant.

I appreciate what Charles Spurgeon says about trials: "Trials teach us what we are; they dig up the soil, and let us see what we are made of."[4] I would never have asked for any of these trials, but I know that my faith was strengthened as I was forced to release control and trust God in each circumstance. My Christian faith was surely tested during this season, but as an old song says, "The anchor holds."

God has allowed me to go through many trials, and I am still learning to consider it all joy (James 1:2-3). I told our executive team on several occasions that I believe God has allowed us to experience many challenges to strengthen, grow, and mature each of us. I am pleased to say that we have learned and continue to learn about His best path forward. We are all a work in progress this side of Heaven!

The lawsuit took a couple of years to resolve, but with a lot of prayer and persistence, we were able to reach an agreement that allowed us to shake hands and part ways. Our house was restored after the Harvey flood. Nikki's mother made it through breast cancer surgery and a year of chemo and is now doing well. With the help of an investigative firm we connected with, through C12 and our insurance company, we were able to replace the funds embezzled from Gulf Winds. We were able to manage through COVID and position the company well going into 2021.

But the most gratifying part of this journey is seeing our now twenty-two-year-old daughter thriving! Lexi now has her own wedding photography business (@lexigracephoto). She is married to Landon, a strong believer, and we have a beautiful granddaughter named Wren! Lexi has learned to deal with the abuse that led to her depression, anxiety, and other challenges, including questioning God's love for her. On her eighteenth birthday, she decided to post a brief part of her story

---

[4] *The Complete Works of C. H. Spurgeon*, vol. 2: Sermons 54–106 (Delmarva Publications, 2015), 233, quoted on *The Pastor's Workshop*, https://thepastorsworkshop.com/quotes/charles-haddon-spurgeon-trials-teach-us-what-we-are-they-dig-id_8886.

on Instagram in an effort to raise money for a nonprofit that helps victims of sex trafficking. She received a tremendous response, and God is now using her story for good as she shares how He can bring healing and restoration to abuse survivors.

The joy of officiating my daughter Lexi's wedding and sharing this sweet family moment!

Lexi recently gave me a Christmas gift: a painting of us walking together, viewed from behind. The caption reads, *"Thank you for being there for me in the valley and tears and on the mountain, smiling. You're my number one man. I love you."* We have watched God literally restore her before our eyes through fervent prayer, the help of an amazing Christian  therapist, a lot of love from us, and an awesome group of Christian friends from church. God really does walk with us in the valleys of life, and the beauty of the journey is that now we can look back on these

Delivering Hope

seasons and know He never wastes any trial or test. God is faithful! He will never leave us nor forsake us.

The mission of leading a business and ministry to success and significance is a calling that takes commitment and support. I have had both from my family and team at Gulf Winds, and I am forever grateful for that. Despite all the challenges that we have faced, there is nothing sweeter than the fruit grown in the difficulties of life for the sake of Christ and His mission. One of the beautiful things about God taking us through these trials is that we can now share and encourage others in their time of need! Every trial is an opportunity to trust the Lord and serve others with His love and grace!

I have journeyed through the long dark night
Out on the open sea, by faith alone
Sight unknown;
And yet His eyes were watching me
The anchor holds
Though the ship is battered

The anchor holds
Though the sails are torn
I have fallen on my knees
As I face the raging seas
The anchor holds in spite of the storm

I've had visions, I've had dreams
I've even held them in my hand
But I never knew they would slip right through
Like they were only grains of sand

The anchor holds
Though the ship is battered

Todd Stewart

The anchor holds
Though the sails are torn
I have fallen on my knees
As I face the raging seas
The anchor holds in spite of the storm

I have been young
But I am older now
And there has been beauty these eyes have seen
But it was in the night, through the storms[5]

Questions to Consider

1. Have you truly counted the cost of leading?
2. What trials are you facing currently that you need to trust the Lord with?
3. How has Lexi's story encouraged you today?
4. How can James 1:2–4 encourage you today?

---

[5] Ray Bolz, "The Anchor Holds," track 8 on *Allegiance*, Word Records, released 1994, CD.

Chapter 8
Take a Trip with God!

"For we are His workmanship, created in Christ Jesus for good works, which God prepared beforehand, that we should walk in them."
—Ephesians 2:10 (ESV)

In early 2010, I was attending a 6:30 a.m. Bible study at the YMCA in our community. One particular day, we had a guest speaker, Mike Roth, who was introducing us to a quickly expanding Christian nonprofit called ICM (International Cooperating Ministries). ICM was founded by a highly successful sixty-five-year-old businessman from Virginia named Dois Rosser, who had been touched deeply by a midweek, application-based Bible study Pastor Dick Woodward had taught for businessmen in the 1980s. The teaching so transformed his life that Rosser wanted to figure out how to get Woodward's teaching to the whole world.

Rosser had been in church for many years and had a lot of Bible knowledge, but he had always separated business from spiritual matters. Woodward showed him there actually is no divide; that was a catalytic moment for Rosser that has resulted in millions of people hearing the Gospel and being discipled globally. Rosser met with Woodward and quickly got into the business of getting the whole Word of God to the whole world by leveraging Christian partners in various countries, starting in India, to rapidly multiply local church plants, then support them with life-changing Bible study materials.

I fell in love with ICM's multiplication model, and Mike Roth and I became friends and ministry partners immediately. I later got the opportunity to meet Dois Rosser and Dick Woodward and joined the ICM board.

Dois Rosser, founder of ICM

Mom, Dad, Nikki, and I with Dois Rosser, his wife Shirley, and daughter Janice (now CEO of ICM) at a Rock award celebration in Virginia, 2014

Shortly thereafter, Gulf Winds used personal and business profits to fund a few new churches and children's Hope Centers in Central and South America. To date, this for-profit/nonprofit partnership has resulted in more than 237 projects in 36 countries impacting more than 50,000 people—and counting!

ICM is all about leveraging resources to expand the Kingdom of God through the local church; It draws alongside indigenous partners who covenant to plant five new congregations within three years for every church building ICM funds—so you can imagine how quickly the

Delivering Hope

church expands in those nations through this leveraged model. Gulf Winds' projects have now established 716 daughter congregations and more than 6,077 discipleship groups! We won't know the full impact of these Kingdom investments until we get to Heaven, but I am looking forward to that celebration!

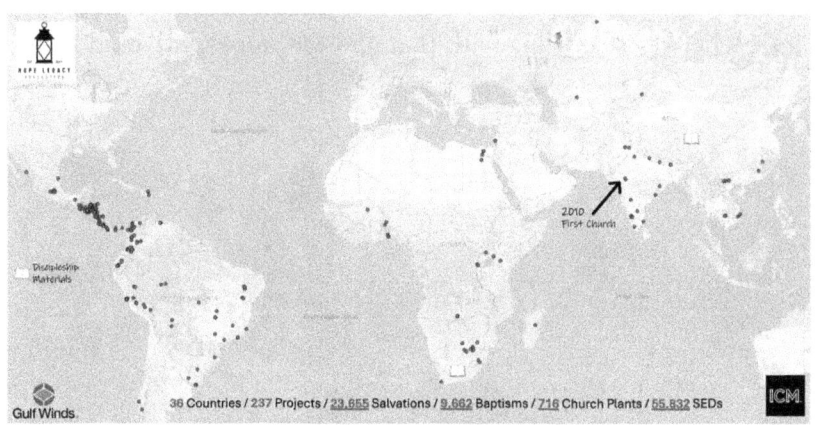

Marketplace ministry kingdom impact through Gulf Winds' partnership with ICM, 2010–2024

Not long after Gulf Winds made its first few gifts, we decided we needed to take a vision trip to Colombia to see firsthand how the ICM model was working there. Vision trips are short-term trips that allow financial supporters to visit projects, hear first-hand testimony about how God is working, and meet the indigenous partners in the field. I had no idea how impactful these vision trips would become over the next several years. God has used them to transform many people's lives and perspectives.

I made a list of people I thought should go with us on that first trip, starting with a key team member, as well as an old high school friend named Mike Morrison, who had become a Gulf Winds customer. The back story on Mike is important. He and I had lunch one day after I realized he was working for a client of ours; I wanted to find out where he was spiritually. I was focused on reaching him with the Gospel, knowing we both had been far from God during high school and college. Our first lunch meeting was enjoyable, but it did not yield spiritual fruit. A month or two later, I still had Mike on my mind for some reason that only God knew, so I reached out to him once again. That time, I asked him how he was doing; I could tell he was in a challenging situation. He told me that his wife was leaving him and they were headed for divorce. Clearly, he was struggling with that and the impact it would have on their son.

ICM vision trip to Colombia, 2012

At the end of our call, I was convicted to ask him to lunch once again, and told him I wanted to share what God had done in my life. He agreed, and a few days later I picked him up from his office and we went to a local restaurant, where I cut right to the chase. I shared how God

Delivering Hope

had worked in my life to lead me into a personal saving relationship with Jesus Christ and the peace I had found by trusting in His death, burial, and resurrection. I took time to explain the Gospel in more detail, specifically what it means to truly submit your life to the Lord and be saved apart from good works, which do not result in salvation.

> *"For by grace you have been saved through faith. And this is not your own doing, it is the gift of God, not a result of works, so that no one may boast."*
> —Ephesians 2:8–9 (ESV)

Mike listened intently, and we talked for the better part of an hour. I drove him back to his office after lunch, and when I pulled into the parking lot, I asked if he would like to openly confess his sins and trust Jesus Christ as his Lord and Savior. In tears, Mike received God's call on his life that day and became a Christian. What are the odds that after fifteen years, I would cross paths with an old high school friend just when he was going through a very difficult time, who just happened to be working for one of our customers? God's timing never ceases to amaze me.

Gulf Winds at the grand opening of a Hope Center in El Salvador, 2016; one of the children served at our Hope Center in Bolivia, 2014

Todd Stewart

So Mike joined us on that trip to Colombia, and it was amazing beyond anything I had imagined! We all experienced the love and power of God firsthand at every church and children's Hope Center we visited. We heard testimonies from kids who had been abused and neglected, about God's love being poured out in their lives through ICM projects.

Hope Centers are similar to American day care centers in the sense that small children in developing countries also need care when both parents are at work, but unlike American day care centers, ICM partners build facilities mainly in poverty-stricken areas. The Hope Centers are overseen by, and often connected to, the local church and serve a very important role in poor communities: feeding and educating children in places where childcare is nonexistent.

A sweet child served by a Hope Center in Brazil, 2019

Erica singing "My Blue House"

The first Hope Center we visited was called "the Blue House," because it was bright blue and stood out on the poor mountainside community surrounding the city of Medellín, the home of a famous drug cartel that ruled the area from the early 1970s to the early 1990s. Erica, the lady who founded the Blue House, had been kidnapped in her early teens and held in a forced relationship by a local drug lord. That is still common practice for those running drugs in the region, and it is a terrifying prospect for parents and young girls in Medellín. By the grace of God, Erica escaped that life a few years later, when her captor was killed in a drug war. Today, she works in the city but spends all her free

Delivering Hope

time with the children at the Hope Center. She has even recruited other family members to support the work!

Children from the Blue House singing "Jesus Loves the Little Children" to welcome us

When we arrived at the Blue House for the first time, we could hear the kids singing "Jesus Loves the Little Children" in English. They were lining the steep stairway that led up the side of the mountain to the center, and they were filled with joy!

Had it not been for the love of Christ that Erica and the other caregivers were sharing with them, though, most of those children would not have had much joy to speak of. Many of the young girls at the center that day spoke of being effectively orphaned when their parents had to leave the area in order to find work. These young girls were often abused physically and sexually. One said she was abused by her father, who would chase her with a machete at times when she would not comply with his wishes.

Joy-filled children welcomed us to their home, the Blue House, in Colombia, 2012.

Another lady named Maria shared her story of abuse and how she had fallen into prostitution to provide for her family. As if that was not bad enough, she received a call one night from someone saying that her daughter had been murdered—and then dismembered. As a father, I can't imagine the pain and suffering this woman lives with. But she told us how Jesus Christ and the local church had rescued her in her time of need. She now serves the local ICM church regularly and spends a lot of time witnessing to people about Jesus on her bus rides around the city. Truly, God can bring restoration and healing to broken people in the most challenging situations.

After a few hours of hearing testimonies like those, there wasn't a dry eye in the place. God was stirring the heart of each man on that trip, letting us know that our work, and the way we partner with ICM churches and Hope Centers, is having a huge impact in places that desperately need hope. When we use business profits for Kingdom work, we have the opportunity to exponentially impact the world in a positive way!

Heartbreaking testimonies at the Blue House softened by the rescuing, redeeming love of God

BJ Tarver, former president, COO, and eventually CEO of Gulf Winds, told me later on that trip that he was deeply convicted personally that funding ICM projects through our company was desperately needed. God was breaking our hearts for His purposes in the world and revealing where we had been selfish and calloused. Our hearts were broken for the things of God on that trip, and that is an awesome and challenging place to be!

Meanwhile, Mike connected with a woman named Carolina who was serving as one of our translators on this trip, and they stayed in touch after he returned home. That grew into a long-distance relationship, and a few years later, they were married.

> *When we use business profits for Kingdom work, we have the opportunity to exponentially impact the world in a positive way!*

They now have two beautiful children together and are serving the Lord! God not only saved Mike and comforted him through his challenging divorce, but also provided him with a godly wife and family. Truly, God does meet us in our time of need when we go on mission with Him. He still actively works miracles, and we can see them when we follow Him and become part of His plan and purpose in the world.

Jeff, Sean, and Mike (left to right), my schoolmates, with their wives Kristy, Candice, and Carolina at A Sheltered Life fundraiser for ICM and a Boys and Girls Country home in Houston

Mike managed to convince two of our other high school friends, Jeff Montgomery and Sean Wheat, to join us on that trip. Neither Jeff nor Sean had ever been on a mission trip of any sort. But by the time we returned home, they had been so deeply impacted by God's work in Colombia that they and Mike formed a nonprofit called A Sheltered Life and began holding annual events to raise money to plant children's Hope Centers through ICM. As of 2024, A Sheltered Life has raised more than 1.5 million dollars to fund local and international ministry efforts

Delivering Hope

through ICM and the Boys and Girls Country of Houston (a home for children), demonstrating God's love to kids around the globe!

A couple of years later, we took another ICM vision trip to El Salvador. Much as in Colombia, there are challenges related to poverty, gangs, and drug issues. That time, I felt I should invite another friend from high school, Eric Anderson, who was involved in a sports ministry called the Fellowship of Christian Athletes (FCA). He had never been out of the country on a mission trip before, so he was very hesitant—so hesitant, in fact, that he turned us down. But I really felt God wanted Eric on the trip, so we removed all barriers for him by paying his way. All we needed from him was a yes—there was no investment required except his time. So he went! Sometimes we must work to remove barriers to bring people along on our God journeys.

My brother in Christ, Eric Anderson, on mission with us in El Salvador (2015); Eric preaching at the Global Outreach Community Church he planted in Humble, Texas to reach the nations!

Eric had a wonderful time on the trip and connected with people at every stop. Shortly after we returned home, Eric was asked to be FCA's international coordinator! While Eric would work from Houston, his new role would take him back to El Salvador many times over the next few years. The ICM trip opened his eyes and heart and prepared him for the opportunity to lead the FCA ministry in Central America. As of 2024, Eric has served in twenty different countries and has been on fifty mission trips; in addition, he has planted the Global Outreach

Community Church in Humble, Texas. You can't make this stuff up! When we are obedient to God's call on our lives, He moves mountains and extends His love and grace through us in ways we would never imagine!

Another friend who took that trip, Robert Walker, was someone I had met at a weekly marketplace Bible study I was leading some time previously. We dove into the Scriptures together and very quickly connected as brothers in the faith. Robert and his boss, Toby Potter, took several ICM trips with us and built quite a few churches and Hope Centers along the way; they later founded another nonprofit to raise money to build churches and Hope Centers, led by contributions from their company.

Pastor Robert Walker and his wife, Jennifer, along with Nikki and I; on mission in the Dominican Republic, 2024

Robert was so convicted of the importance of the local church and the purity with which we saw materially impoverished people worshiping Jesus overseas that he and his wife, Jennifer, felt led to start a home church, The Prayer Room Church in Conroe, Texas. It has since outgrown the Walkers' house, and many lives have been impacted for the Kingdom. We like to think of The Prayer Room as the first ICM church on U.S. soil! The church has gone on to lead twenty mission trips over the last ten years! It's amazing how God multiplies our efforts when we follow His leading to *go* on mission for His Glory!

Delivering Hope

Pastor Walker baptizing his wife, Jennifer, at the home church they founded in Conroe, Texas

Questions to Consider

1. Have you ever taken a short-term mission or vision trip? Why or why not?
2. How have these stories encouraged and challenged you to take a trip with God?
3. What obstacles do you need to ask God to remove so you can take a trip with Him?

Chapter 9
The Bus Ride and Defining Moments

> *"And Jesus came and said to them, 'All authority in heaven and on earth has been given to me. Go and make disciples of all nations, baptizing them in the name of the Father and the Son and of the Holy Spirit, teaching them to observe all that I have commanded you. And behold, I am with you always, to the end of the age.'"*
> —Matthew 28:18–20 (ESV)

After just a few vision trips with ICM, we realized the power of taking others on a journey with God. After flying into the destination country, we usually travel by bus with amazing translators who become like family as we travel between churches and children's Hope Centers, seeing and hearing powerful testimonies of God's grace and soul-moving praise and worship at each location. The idea is to *put people in a position to hear from God* and then watch and celebrate what happens as a result of that encounter.

I've taken my family on many short-term mission trips, starting when our kids were in elementary school. Mission trips are so impactful that I always recommend bringing family members and/or friends to enjoy and help digest the experience, not only while in the country, but also upon your return.

Gulf Winds men on mission in El Salvador, 2015

Going alone can lead to unforeseen challenges when you return. We are simply better together in the kingdom of God. The impact and life change you will experience through God's presence and the testimony of His work is exponential, and it's difficult, if not impossible, to explain.

Jamie Hampton, Executive Director of Gulf Winds' Hope Legacy Collective Foundation (formerly More Than the Move) with Lane in Costa Rica—vision trip 2019

Delivering Hope

My son, Lane, went on many trips with us from the time he was very young, and he continues to go every chance he gets. To date, Lane has been to over thirty-five countries, and at age twenty-four, God has gifted him with a missions internship at United City Church in Humble, Texas, beginning August 2025. I have no doubt in my mind that our prayers that God would use him powerfully largely influenced God's work in his life, but the short-term mission trips he experienced growing up definitely did too. Young people are desperate for purpose and meaning in our broken world. The Gospel can be experienced powerfully on mission trips and can provide needed perspective to young and old alike!

Lane preaching at the Prayer Room church in Conroe, Texas, 2024; Supporting my son in ministry brings so much joy to my heart (October 2024)

Over the years, the people I've included on these trips have expanded from immediate friends and family to employees and their friends and family. When we asked Gulf Winds team members in 2012 if they wanted to travel with us, we were pleasantly surprised to find out how excited they were about it. Over the next few years, we managed to take a large percentage of our employees and their spouses, or children, on vision trips. We usually schedule a couple of them each year, and we draw names to see who gets to go. I have taken my wife, son, and daughter on multiple vision trips, and I am certain that our family's ministry focus and Christian worldview have been enhanced exponentially by experiencing the love of God's people and life-changing testimony around the globe. When you meet people with very little, materially, who love the Lord and worship with their full heart, mind, and soul despite their challenging circumstances, you can't help but be encouraged.

Above left: Ania & Luke Greenwood (European leaders for Steiger International) with Lane, Nikki, and I in Germany at Steiger's missions school, 2024; top right: Jamie Hampton, along with Whitney Brown, former Gulf Winds' employee, and her mom in Panama on an ICM vision trip, 2020; bottom right: One person can change a life! Nikki and I in Peru, 2014

Delivering Hope

On every trip, there seems to be a defining moment that removes all pretense and connects us deeply to one another. On a trip to Bolivia a few years back, we were on a bus heading to a remote indigenous Bolivian village to visit a new ICM church when we got caught in a flash flood. As someone who grew up operating boats, I recognized the "wake" in the water behind our bus and figured that was not good. We arrived at our destination, but the rain was not subsiding, and the floodwaters were rolling over the road and submerging the field beside us. At that point, we had to decide: Would we stay on the bus and play it safe, or get out of the bus and wade through knee-deep water to the church building

God rescues and saves, in us and through us! Preaching in Bolivia, 2014

approximately two hundred yards away? One passenger was in tears, and I felt the pressure of ensuring everyone's well-being. Thankfully, with some encouragement, we managed to talk everyone into getting off the bus.

After wading for some time through the floodwaters, we arrived at the church, where we were met by singers and dancers in full indigenous dress. We entered the church and worshiped through song and dance together, and had an amazing time. God had come through again! Our whole group bonded in that difficult situation, and the rest of the trip was off the charts! Serving the Lord is not easy, but He is faithful to see us through challenging circumstances. Often, there is great blessing on the other side of obstacles for those who walk in obedience and do not cower in fear. *"Have I not commanded you? Be strong and courageous. Do not be frightened, and do not be dismayed, for the Lord your God is with you wherever you go"* (Joshua 1:9 ESV).

Later on that trip, I celebrated my fortieth birthday by preaching at a church about Jesus calming the storm, figuring that was fitting after our brush with death in the Bolivian floodwaters. The response from the church—which was celebrating its fortieth anniversary—was amazing. Many people came forward to receive the gift of salvation, and I could really feel the Spirit moving in the hearts of people.

I was standing in front of the altar, explaining to a young couple the salvation message and leading them in prayer, when my translator, a Gulf Winds employee, looked at me with a tear in her eye and said, "Me too." God had done it again! Through translating the Word I was preaching, God had broken her heart for the Gospel, and she received salvation as well!

"So faith comes from hearing, and hearing through the word of Christ."
—Romans 10:17 (ESV)

One thing we enjoy most about international vision trips is the incredible ways in which God works in the hearts and lives of those who go. I must admit that after the first trip, I doubted God. I did not doubt who He was, but I doubted that the amazing impact we saw on that trip could be replicated. I have been proven wrong over and over, as God does immeasurably more than we could ever hope or imagine every time. Inevitably, people's perspectives are radically impacted, and God transforms their hearts and minds. He has taught us that if we can just get people to take the bus ride, He will take care of the rest. It is not up to us to change hearts, but we are tasked with inviting people to go on this amazing journey!

Taking a mission or vision trip is very humbling. Below are testimonials from employees who have taken trips with us.

Delivering Hope

"My biggest takeaway was being able ... to see how fulfilling it is to help others. As a kid, I received help from missionaries, and to be in their place really gave me a sense of purpose."

"I was amazed at the magnitude of faith, love, and hope the people we met had. They were so gracious despite having so little, and it was really encouraging. My takeaways are to continue to make efforts to pursue the Lord before anything else, and actively seek out ways I can impact someone's life, whether it's in monetary donations, time spent volunteering, connecting with people, or words of encouragement."

"This experience was soul-changing. I will never be the same."

"This trip has truly changed me in a way that I can't even describe. My heart has been forever touched by all the people we have met, and especially the children. I will hold on to these memories for a lifetime."

"This experience made me face some issues I had bottled in. The people were amazing!!! It definitely opened my eyes and heart."

"At first, I was not sure if I wanted to go, but honestly ... all the love I felt from people I have never seen before was amazing. God presents Himself to you in many ways, and this was His way of letting me know He loves me."

"The main takeaway was how the churches worshiped. They didn't care where they were. They just wanted to serve God. It made me open up my eyes. I believe in God, but when it comes to going to church, I always make excuses for why I can't go. But when I saw those kids and adults worshiping in the mountains, under tarps, in buildings with no air [conditioning] or windows, it made me see how

good we have it in the U.S. and how much we take it for granted. This trip has definitely gotten me closer to God. Getting to know my teammates on a deeper level was also great."

"I will always remember this trip as [one] that helped me reconnect with God and put a lot of things in perspective in the way I live my life."

"It was an extremely powerful feeling how STRONG God's presence and love was in all of the places we visited. It is difficult to find the right words to explain it!"

Questions to Consider

1. Who do you need to invite on an international mission or vision trip?
2. What defining moments in your life opened your eyes to the love of God?
3. What challenging circumstance do you need to push through to experience more of God's love, grace, mercy, and provision?

Chapter 10
More Than the Move

"Whatever you do, work heartily, as for the Lord and not for men, knowing that from the Lord you will receive the inheritance as your reward. You are serving the Lord Christ."
—Colossians 3:23–24 (ESV)

After my father passed away in January 2017, God put it on my heart to start a foundation to put a structure around all our philanthropic work. What we do at Gulf Winds is about more than moving freight, so our marketing slogan is "More than the move." We want our employees to know that the work they do each day matters and has a greater purpose. "More Than the Move" seemed like a perfect name for the foundation I wanted to start, so we launched with great expectation that this was the beginning of something great. Through volunteering, giving, and social media marketing, More Than the Move supports local and international nonprofit partners that restore hope in the lives of people. Our foundation delivers what nonprofits need: encouragement, prayer, financial support, and volunteers.

By that point, Gulf Winds had been doing a lot of charitable work. We were designating a portion of our profits each month toward life-changing local and international nonprofits to restore hope in the lives of people; we also had established a compassion fund to help Gulf Winds team members in need.

Gulf Winds' headquarters in Houston

I was very encouraged that the daily work of our team was making a true positive impact in the world by providing resources to fight human trafficking, support crisis pregnancy centers, drill water wells in developing countries, educate children, help veterans, support homeless shelters, feed those in need, plant churches, and grow sports ministries that were reaching many student athletes in and around Houston.

Through More Than the Move (now Hope Legacy Collective), Gulf Winds is restoring hope to people's lives locally and across the globe!

Delivering Hope

We hired marketplace chaplains to visit with our team members on-site a couple of times a month to provide an outlet for them to share any personal, professional, or spiritual needs. More than fifty of our Gulf Winds team members had experienced personally the joy of traveling internationally at our expense with ICM to see the life-changing work done at the children's Hope Centers and churches we had planted in Central and South America. Whole communities in developing countries were being restored through our faithful corporate giving. We provided good pay, benefits, and 401(k) matching, along with profit sharing when the company could afford it. On paper, we were a model C12 company doing incredible things for the Kingdom of God—but something was missing.

Hope Legacy backpack giveaway supporting Houston schoolchildren

In mid-2017, our executive team decided to launch our first anonymous company-wide employee engagement survey to get a true picture of how our leaders were doing. The survey confirmed that we still had quite a bit of room to grow in the area of employee engagement.

Despite all the wonderful things we were doing, some areas of the company scored much lower than we had hoped. Our overall score was 52 percent, which is still well above the national average, but I was deeply concerned that half of our employees were not engaged. Our management team did a wonderful job of addressing problem areas and really listening to our employees. All of our giving was great, but giving apart from hands-on service left a void that had to be bridged if we were to connect our employees to the greater purpose of Gulf Winds and More Than the Move.

As noted, we started the More Than the Move Foundation with the idea of restoring hope locally and globally by serving and giving financial resources to local and international nonprofits. We bridge the gap between the for-profit and nonprofit worlds and, in the process, connect people to a greater purpose. As it turned out, however, a byproduct of purposefully connecting our team members with service opportunities in their area of passion was increased employee engagement.

Jamie Hampton and I at Niagara Falls, Canada, where I spoke on workplace ministry at the GO Conference, 2019

The idea gained momentum quickly, and we appointed a young man named Jamie Hampton to be the foundation's executive director and help connect our employees' passions to the work we were doing. Jamie had worked briefly in operations for Gulf Winds before transferring to our business development division—but more importantly, he had spent time serving in college ministry, and his caring and compassionate heart was very evident to all our employees.

Shortly thereafter, we surveyed our employees to find out which of the twenty nonprofits we were working with in the Houston area

Delivering Hope

matched their areas of passion or interest. We already had a great list of fantastic hope-restoring organizations in Houston that we had been supporting, so it only took a little follow-up work to determine and schedule volunteer opportunities for our employees. The result was fantastic, and when combined with the wonderful work of our executive team and directors, who were focused on job-specific employee engagement, we were able to raise our engagement scores by nearly 40 percent to an industry-leading and best-in-class 71 percent in just six months! We also managed to meet our volunteer time goal of four thousand hours that year!

I learned as a ministry-minded servant leader that we could do a lot of great things as an organization in the areas of giving and ministry, but if our team members were not *personally connected to or interested in those things* in some way, we were missing out on a wonderful engagement opportunity. In addition, if we had not addressed job-specific issues, we would have had a hard time connecting team members to a greater purpose.

> *If we had not addressed job-specific issues, we would have had a hard time connecting team members to a greater purpose.*

Hope Legacy volunteers packing meals for local children with Kids' Meals in Houston; Hope Legacy Volunteer Day

For our first major foundation volunteer event, we decided to partner with a nonprofit that provides the tools for groups to pack mass quantities of meals for those in need. The event was a huge success! We managed to partner with many other companies in our industry, as well as a few clients and vendors, to package 100,000 meals in one day, which were distributed by the Houston Food Bank. I am reminded of Jesus' words in Mark 6:

> *But he answered them, 'You give them something to eat.' And they said to him, 'Shall we go and buy two hundred denarii worth of bread and give it to them to eat?' And he said to them, 'How many loaves do you have? Go and see.' And when they had found out, they said, 'Five, and two fish.' Then he commanded them all to sit down in groups on the green grass. So they sat down in groups, by hundreds and by fifties. And taking the five loaves and the two fish, he looked up to heaven and said a blessing and broke the loaves and gave them to the disciples to set before the people. And he divided the two fish among them all. And they all ate and were satisfied. And they took up twelve baskets full of broken pieces and of the fish. And those who ate the loaves were five thousand men.* (vv. 37–44 ESV)

A Gulf Winds' team tackling hunger in Houston at our first large Hope Legacy event!

It is truly amazing what can be accomplished when people work together to meet the needs of others without caring who gets the credit.

Delivering Hope

God really does bless these service ventures in amazing ways. A key element to the success of our first event was that we all came together under one banner. We even had competitors join us to pack meals that day. Service events for the greater good create cooperation and unity even amongst rivals.

After our first few volunteer events, we realized quickly that this service model could be scaled far beyond Gulf Winds. So we partnered with several other C12 companies to run a network of "employee cares" volunteer programs through what we now call the Hope Legacy Collective, to better represent all of the companies involved. We are excited to see how God will continue to multiply finances and volunteers as we pool our collective resources to restore hope in our community and the world, leaving a legacy beyond business success.

One volunteer opportunity that sticks with me to this day is the story of a young couple I met at a Houston children's hospital, where our employees had set up a Mexican buffet to feed the children's families. I spoke briefly to a young couple in the line—Callie and Blake—who turned out to be from Nacogdoches, Texas. I connected with them immediately, since Nacogdoches is the location of Stephen F. Austin University, my alma mater. I learned they had a baby named Kannon who had been delivered six weeks prematurely and was very sick. Kannon's doctors had given him a 0 percent chance of living. I couldn't even keep up with all the medical issues Callie outlined for me—I only knew to pray.

After dinner and prayer, I told her and Blake I would follow up with them if they didn't mind. They welcomed the prayer and support. Miraculously, Kannon made it and was released from the hospital a few months later. The family wound up moving into a small apartment not far from where I live. Jamie Hampton and I stopped by to see them one day and discovered that their only transportation was an old farm truck that had no air conditioning and more than 400,000 miles on it.

Kannon could not ride with no AC because of all his breathing complications, so we quickly sent a request for help through our network. To our joy, a friend from C12 who also has a special-needs daughter told us he was about to trade in his car, and this young family could have it! We later wound up partnering with another C12 member who owns and operates an automotive dealership to get Callie and Blake a newer car, and we were able to raise enough money to pay for a few months' rent as well.

In short, through a quick service opportunity to feed some folks at a hospital, God literally provided life-saving transportation and provision for a special-needs child and restored hope for this family. *We really are better together.*

Our goal at the Hope Legacy Collective is to link with the hands and resources of small and mid-sized businesses, to fund and serve life-changing nonprofits, and restore hope in people's lives by the grace of God! I can't think of anything more rewarding than being the hands and feet of Jesus!

The following are actual testimonials from people who have served with us locally at More than the Move and Hope Legacy Collective.

"I learned to be grateful to God for everything and that we need to stretch out a helping hand where we can. Thank you."

"It feels good to be able to give back to the community."

"I feel very fortunate to have volunteered with colleagues from Panalpina and Gulf Winds. As homeless people were being served a warm meal, you could feel the energy in the room. The people were very kind and generally grateful despite what each was going through personally. We have to give the homeless hope and not give up. I feel humbled. When I returned to the office, I started planning on volunteering again with my team, who did not have this opportunity."

"Giving your time to help others is a wonderful experience."

Delivering Hope

"I loved being involved in a volunteer activity that was family-friendly. Being able to impact the community where we live and work and explain to the kids why it is so important to take care of our environment was such a wonderful experience. Thanks!"

"Volunteering at the Beach Clean Up was a great experience for our whole family. Our kids were so excited to volunteer and learned firsthand the repercussions of littering. Serving others has brought our family closer together and allowed us as adults to lead by example."

"It reminded me how the Scriptures tell us to take care of the widows and the orphans. Considering most of the elderly here are widows, it made me ask myself if I'm being obedient to the Scriptures in this matter."

"I hope we impacted the women's and children's lives as much as they impacted us. I walked out of there speaking about my experience with anyone who would listen."

"I loved helping those who need our help. We can't do it on our own."

"I learned how the little things make a difference. Seeing one lady open the door and cry as I handed her a rose and wished her a happy Mother's Day just made me say, 'Wow, what has she been through?' I just had to give her a hug and let her know how much we were all so glad to be there for her and the other ladies at the Bridge!"

"Awareness. I have always wanted to volunteer, but was not sure how. After my visit, I have the tools to get involved."

"I learned you can have an impact on so many kids' lives in one day. Also, some of these kids could use the attention to help them realize how great they are."

"This is where my heart lies, being able to reach out to children, bring them joy. What an amazing experience and a huge blessing to be able to partake in making a difference. Thank you MTTM for allowing us to be a part of that day."

"Doing God's work is always a way to heal your faith in humanity. Giving back to others the love the Lord gives us is a wonderful feeling."

"It was very rewarding to help other people."

"I learned we are all able to use our gifts and talents—regardless of how small we may think they are. It is OK to step out of your comfort zone, as nobody is perfect."

Questions to Consider

1. Would you consider joining our collective movement to restore hope in people's lives?
2. Why is it important to link people's passions with service opportunities?
3. How were you encouraged by God's provision in Kannon's story and the other testimonials?
4. How can you use your business profits and team members to support life-changing nonprofit work in your area?

Chapter 11
The Importance of Unity

"So if there is any encouragement in Christ, any comfort from love, any participation in the Spirit, any affection and sympathy, complete my joy by being of the same mind, having the same love, being in full accord and of one mind. Do nothing from selfish ambition or conceit, but in humility count others more significant than yourselves. Let each of you look not only to his own interests, but also to the interests of others."
—Philippians 2:1–4 (ESV)

Shortly after I took over as president at Gulf Winds, I found myself spending a significant amount of time in the book of Nehemiah. This is a wonderful leadership book that I had been through several times before, but at that time, it became especially meaningful. I was in charge and knew I needed a team of people who not only supported me, but who were unified in the mission, vision, and values of our company.

Even more importantly, I needed people who could execute all those things in the marketplace—which meant they also had to live them out in their personal lives. Simply put, there was no way we could operate as we needed to at Gulf Winds apart from having men and women who reflected our values of humility, compassion, integrity, stewardship, and excellence throughout our company.

The Gulf Winds family: opportunity in the making!

The first chapter of Nehemiah is crucial to the entire book because it reveals the prophet's heart toward God, his own sin, his people, and the city of Jerusalem. After hearing a bad report about the desperate condition of his homeland, Nehemiah's character as a leader is displayed.

The Heart of the Leader

"As soon as I heard these words, I sat down and wept and mourned for days, and I continued fasting and praying before the God of heaven."
—Nehemiah 1:4 (ESV)

Nehemiah goes on to confess the moral failings of the people of Israel, understanding that apart from brutal honesty, they had no hope of redemption and restoration. As leaders, we need to have the heart of Nehemiah—and in the words of my late friend and author Pastor Dick Woodward, we must "organize, deputize, and most importantly agonize as leaders." Agonizing is the most difficult part, in my view, because it speaks to the physical and mental toll that leadership takes on people.

After prayer and confession, Nehemiah petitions the Lord for success in rebuilding the walls of Jerusalem. He realizes that the only way he will be able to escape his captivity in Babylon and get the blessing, provision, and protection of King Artaxerxes to go back to his homeland and accomplish that task is by the hand of God. As a Christian leader, I desire blessing, provision, and protection from the Lord, so this model is ideal.

Since 2012, I have spent a considerable amount of time organizing, deputizing, and agonizing over the team we have at Gulf Winds. I have had to make difficult decisions to build and tear down and start over a few times. I am incredibly thankful for the diverse mix of talent throughout our company. It takes a great deal of humility to maintain a spirit of unity on any team, and ours is no different. God's Word speaks to the value of humility in creating a culture of unity.

The Value of Humility in Building Unity

> *"I, therefore, a prisoner for the Lord, urge you to walk in a manner worthy of the calling to which you have been called, with all humility and gentleness, with patience, bearing with one another in love, eager to maintain the unity of the Spirit in the bond of peace."*
> *—Ephesians 4:1–3 (ESV)*

We must fight for unity daily. My heart's desire for our team is that their varied gifts and talents would be multiplied throughout our company for God's glory and Gulf Winds' success. A plethora of giftings is a blessing on any team, and should be recognized as such.

The Gulf Winds family at our 20th anniversary luncheon, 2016

Todd Stewart

The Value of Diversity in Offices

Paul outlines this well in Ephesians 4, referring to the value of diversity in the church:

> *And he gave the apostles, the prophets, the evangelists, the shepherds and teachers, to equip the saints for the work of ministry, for building up the body of Christ, until we all attain to the unity of the faith and of the knowledge of the Son of God, to mature manhood, to the measure of the stature of the fullness of Christ, so that we may no longer be children, tossed to and fro by the waves and carried about by every wind of doctrine, by human cunning, by craftiness in deceitful schemes. Rather, speaking the truth in love, we are to grow up in every way into him who is the head, into Christ, from whom the whole body, joined and held together by every joint with which it is equipped, when each part is working properly, makes the body grow so that it builds itself up in love.* (Ephesians 4:11–16 ESV)

I have learned that the most difficult part of any job is managing people with very different personalities and giftings; *only God can truly align the hearts of men and women to accomplish a task for a greater purpose.* Gaining cooperation is wonderful, but maintaining unity requires transparency and humility at every turn. People are the most amazing yet challenging creations in the universe. God created us in His image—and at times we all want to be little gods, if we are honest. Much of our time and resources are focused inwardly instead of outwardly. This is not good, so it is imperative that leaders are humble and transparent in their approach to everything they do and lead. Walls come down one brick at a time, so we need leaders who are willing to remove the first brick and allow others inside their fortresses. I like the song that says, "I'm just a nobody trying to tell everybody about the Somebody that saved my soul."[6] Jesus is our greatest example here.

---

[6] "Nobody," featuring Matthew West, track 2 on Casting Crowns, *Only Jesus*, released 2018, CD.

Christ's Example of Humility

> *So if there is any encouragement in Christ, any comfort from love, any participation in the Spirit, any affection and sympathy, complete my joy by being of the same mind, having the same love, being in full accord and of one mind. Do nothing from selfish ambition or conceit, but in humility count others more significant than yourselves. Let each of you look not only to his own interests, but also to the interests of others. Have this mind among yourselves, which is yours in Christ Jesus, who, though he was in the form of God, did not count equality with God a thing to be grasped, but emptied himself, by taking the form of a servant, being born in the likeness of men. And being found in human form, he humbled himself by becoming obedient to the point of death, even death on a cross. Therefore God has highly exalted him and bestowed on him the name that is above every name, so that at the name of Jesus every knee should bow, in heaven and on earth and under the earth, and every tongue confess that Jesus Christ is Lord, to the glory of God the Father.* (Philippians 2:1–11 ESV)

When it comes to setting up a structure and seeking growth, leaders must learn how to delegate—or else every organization hits a ceiling. It is challenging to consider the reality that we must be willing to give away resources, responsibility, authority, position, and credit in order to grow and expand. From birth, everything in us fights to hang on to these things, *but God's Word teaches us that we must live with an open hand and heart to thrive.*

After careful inspection and taking time to understand the challenges before him, Nehemiah appointed people to help build the wall and guard Jerusalem's city gates. These people were selected based on their skills, and they had a mindset to work and defend the project as well.

Todd Stewart

Leaders Must Guard and Build at the Same Time

"Those who carried burdens were loaded in such a way that each labored on the work with one hand and held his weapon with the other."
—Nehemiah 4:17 (ESV)

I can say with confidence that I have a team that will fight for our mission. Healthy conflict comes with accountability, but when the mission takes priority, it can and does result in personal and professional growth.

Growing together, and ready for any challenge! Gulf Winds, 2018

"Iron sharpens iron, and one man sharpens another."
—Proverbs 27:17 (ESV)

God's work is always opposed by those who wish to tear down rather than build up. Never was this more apparent than in Jesus Christ coming to this earth, living a sin-free life, and being persecuted to the point of death, even death on a cross.

Choosing to run a company on Christian principles and values is challenging in today's culture, but the hope-restoring, eternal benefits, and God's provision far outweigh the challenges. I am reminded of Jesus' words, which speak to the peace found on this journey.

> *"I have said these things to you, that in me you may have peace. In the world you will have tribulation. But take heart; I have overcome the world."*
> —John 16:33 (ESV)

The Wall Is Finished

Nehemiah had a huge task before him, but he knew that through God's power and provision, he would overcome!

> *"So the wall was finished on the twenty-fifth day of the month Elul, in fifty-two days. And when all our enemies heard of it, all the nations around us were afraid and fell greatly in their own esteem, for they perceived that this work had been accomplished with the help of our God."*
> —Nehemiah 6:15–16 (ESV)

Questions to Consider

1. What seemingly impossible task lies before you?
2. How are you encouraged by Nehemiah's approach and God's provision?
3. Why is humility so critical to unity?
4. If Jesus is our example in humility, what can we learn from Philippians 2:1–11?

Chapter 12
Playing the Shuffle

"Do nothing from selfish ambition or conceit, but in humility count others more significant than yourselves."
—Philippians 2:3 (ESV)

My kids always give me a hard time about the way I find lessons in all of life. I can see a dead armadillo and find a life lesson to apply. On that note, I was on a podcast recently and the host asked me about significant lessons I'd learned while growing up. Although I hadn't thought about it in some time, I reflected on one from playing high school football in my senior year.

It was August 1991 in the middle of two-a-day practices in 100-degree Texas summer heat, and I was competing for the starting quarterback job at Humble High School. My main competition, Jeff Orth, and I had battled off and on for the quarterback job since our middle-school days. As we competed for it again that summer, I believed I was the better passer and he was the better runner. We had scrimmaged against Spring High School that year, and at one point, I threw a long touchdown pass to one of our talented receivers for the only score of the game. The papers read, "Orth efficient on the ground and Stewart efficient through the air." I thought I had done enough to win the job, but our head coach wound up going with Jeff and asking me to play free safety on defense. I had never played any position other than quarterback since I started playing football in third grade, but I accepted the position, as I wanted to be on the field for Friday night lights in Texas.

About three or four games into the season, we were approaching one of the biggest games of the year against our archrival, Kingwood High School, just across the river. Kingwood was seen as the upper-class part of town, and Humble was viewed as the working class, so you can imagine how the coaches played that up in our practices before the game. I remember one coach saying, "They drink champagne and we drink beer." They knew how to fuel our fire.

Daryl Anderson, John Forsythe, Larry Harris, and I, Wildcat teammates, 1991

On the Monday before the game, I was sitting in class when there was a knock at the classroom door. It turned out to be our offensive coordinator, who pointed to me and politely asked the teacher if he could speak with me. I met him in the hallway, where he proceeded to tell me that one of our very best offensive players was hurt and he needed me to play running back. Being the backup quarterback, I knew

Delivering Hope

all the plays, so it was a quick fix leading into the big game. While I didn't let it show, I was very nervous and excited at the same time. (Incidentally, the guy I replaced that week went on to play in the NFL for more than ten years.)

Playing the shuffle as a running back (#7)

That Friday, I got the ball on the first play of the game on a 28 sweep and picked up a few yards. That got the butterflies out—and we won the game!

WILDCAT GAIN. Todd Stewart carries the ball for Humble and picks up yardage in the 10-7 victory over Kingwood. — Photo by VICKI PRUETT

The unity of our team brought many victories in our 1991–92 football season.

Todd Stewart

Our team went on to overachieve that season. The papers widely reported early in the season that the class that had gone before us had more talent, primarily because two of the graduating players went on to play Division 1 ball. The difference was that we played as a unit, very unselfishly, and it served us very well. We won a lot of games and upset Beaumont Westbrook in the bi-district playoffs at their home stadium before losing a very close game to a huge Willowridge team in the Houston Astrodome to end the season.

Jamie Polk blocking for me in our game against St. Thomas, fall 1991.
In football and in life, we win as a team.

So what's the lesson in this story? The point is, I was never comfortable that whole season. I was shuffled from quarterback to safety to running back and wedge breaker on the kickoff team. Keep in mind that all I ever played was quarterback from third grade on—but I embraced the discomfort for the sake of my team. At the end of the

Delivering Hope

season, one of my long-time coaches gave me a handwritten note saying how thankful he was for my unselfish play. In addition, after our last home game of the season, one of the other players' dads told me how he thought my willingness to play the shuffle really helped the team.

Sometimes in life, we have to play the shuffle in order to help the team. Life is hard and we do not always get the prize, but there are rewards along the way when we accept whichever role will serve the common good.

> *Sometimes we have to play the shuffle in order to help the team.*

1991–1992 Humble Wildcats senior football team

Questions to Consider

1. Can you identify with my story? If so, how?
2. How can you best help your team, family, or company win?
3. Are you willing to accept another role to see the team succeed?

Chapter 13
The Four Spiritual Secrets

> *"I can't, but He can, and I am in Him and He is in me."*
> *I don't want to, but He wants to, and I am in Him and He is in me.*
> *I didn't, but He did, and I am in Him and He is in me.*
> *I am not, but He is, and I am in Him and He is in me."*
> —Dick Woodward, The 4 Spiritual Secrets

When I first got involved with ICM, I had the joy and privilege of meeting Pastor Dick Woodward in person at his home in Virginia. He was in his eighties at the time, and a degenerative spinal disease had resulted in him becoming fully quadriplegic later in life, but his physical condition did not keep him from serving the Lord. He kept a busy schedule counseling young couples, and was still writing books by speaking into a microphone that recorded his words on his computer. Dick was unable to feed himself or go to the bathroom on his own and required care twenty-four hours a day, but his ministry was still going strong. I will always remember my visits with Dick because he encouraged me so much with his faith in the midst of such a difficult physical condition.

Dick's application-based Bible teaching is what ICM uses with ministry partners all over the globe. The four spiritual secrets he wrote about still encourage me to have faith over fear and to trust the Lord in all seasons of life and business.

As a college student, I reluctantly signed up for a speech class because it was required for a business degree. I remember being terrified to the point of having to go to the bathroom before giving my first speech. As I stood before the class, all alone up there, I realized that the fear of public speaking is very real. I got through my speech, but not without my upper lip shaking uncontrollably from a muscle spasm I had never experienced before! I wound up majoring in marketing, and despite my overwhelming nerves, I excelled in the area of public speaking. In hindsight, I think God was teaching me to trust Him when I was not following Him due to fear. "I can't, but He can, and I am in Him and He is in me."

> *The four spiritual secrets still encourage me to have faith over fear and to trust the Lord in all seasons of life and business. Sometimes you have to play the shuffle in order to help the team.*

After coming to faith at the age of twenty-five, I was asked to share teaching responsibilities for my Sunday school class with a good friend, Billy Russell, who had been a devoted Christian for a few years. At the time, I was really terrified, because I still didn't like getting up in front of people, and I felt ill-equipped to share God's Word since I was just starting to learn it myself. Everything in me said *no* when Billy asked me to help out, but my mouth said, "Yes." I recall those early days of teaching on Sunday as very pressure-packed. I would be up until two o'clock in the morning, trying to read the material and understand it well enough to communicate it to the class. I spent a lot of time on my knees just asking God to help me and to speak through me. God answered my prayers, and I was often encouraged to find teaching as a gift of mine. I suppose that gifting, combined with many hours of study, resulted in a good outcome. It was hard for me, but God used that time in my life to grow me exponentially and to overcome my fear of public speaking. I truly learned to trust God in that season, and He was faithful to work through me to help others and grow me in the process. "I don't want to, but He wants to, and I am in Him and He is in me."

This public-speaking gift became very beneficial at Gulf Winds when I was called upon to speak at industry events—and by God's grace, I was often asked to pray as well! Not only was God teaching me to trust Him more, but He was opening up opportunities for me to be bold and weave His love and grace into whatever marketplace speaking engagements came my way. I always take great joy in including bits of God's truth in every message, no matter the audience. God's Word is powerful, and it reaches the hearts of people.

> *"So shall my word be that goes out from my mouth; it shall not return to me empty, but it shall accomplish that which I purpose, and shall succeed in the thing for which I sent it."*
> —Isaiah 55:11 (ESV)

Chatting with Buck Jacobs, C12 founder, at the C1 Current Conference in Atlanta, Georgia, 2019

In late 2018, I was asked to speak at C12's national conference in Atlanta. God opened the door for me to share the Gulf Winds God story with a room full of 850 Christian CEOs. While I was very nervous before the event, I knew in my heart that God had prepared me for that moment to encourage other Christian businesspeople to use their work as a ministry platform. I remember the C12 CEO, Mike Sharrow, asking me, before I took the stage to kick off the conference, if I was ready. I had spent the whole day in prayer and the Word of God, reading the whole book of John that day. I was *so* ready! I told Mike I believed God had been preparing me for that moment my whole life. What a joy it was to tell God's story and encourage so many that night with the opportunity we have as businesspeople to reach others with the Good News of Jesus Christ in the marketplace. "I didn't, but He did, and I am in Him and He is in me."

I was overwhelmed with encouragement for the next several days at the conference, and I rested in the joy of knowing that God had taken a weakness of mine and turned it into a strength that was used for His glory. As Christ followers, we must be ready to use our gifts for His purposes when called upon to do so, and trust Him for the results.

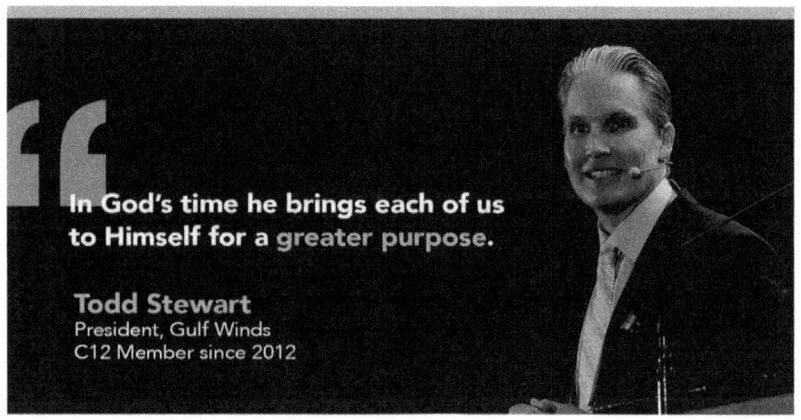

Excerpt from my speech at the C12 Current Conference in Georgia, 2019. True in business and in life!

On one of our ICM trips to El Salvador, I was asked to preach just a few minutes before we arrived at one of the churches we were visiting.

Delivering Hope

Most of those churches are very small. They usually hold approximately two hundred people, maximum. But on that particular Sunday, we were visiting a very large church in one of the major towns. A few minutes later, I found myself in a huge building, standing before several thousand people with my Bible open, preaching through a translator.

God can turn our weakness into strength, and do the impossible!
Preaching in El Salvador, 2015

If you had told me during my sophomore year of college that much of my professional work would involve public speaking engagements and that I would be standing in a church of ten thousand, preaching about Jesus healing a demon-possessed man, I would have told you that you were insane. I am living proof that God can work miracles through His people, and He can do the same in you! "I didn't, but He did, and I am in Him and He is in me."

God does not call the equipped but equips the called, so He gets the credit. One of the most amazing things God will do, on occasion, is take a weakness and make it a significant strength for you. This reality makes the receiver fully dependent on the Lord, which is a wonderful place to be in life. We are never stronger than when we are operating in an area that is dependent on the Lord, not our own strength. "I am not, but He is, and I am in Him and He is in me."

Questions to Consider

1. What fear or insecurity is preventing you from fulfilling God's call on your life?
2. How does hearing how God turned my weakness into a strength encourage you to step out in faith?
3. In what area or situation do you need to rely on God's strength instead of your own?
4. How have the four spiritual secrets encouraged you today?

Chapter 14
Times of Transition

> *"This Book of the Law shall not depart from your mouth, but you shall meditate on it day and night, so that you may be careful to do according to all that is written in it. For then you will make your way prosperous, and then you will have good success."*
> —Joshua 1:8 (ESV)

God knows what His people need to advance His purposes in different seasons of life, and sometimes this requires a transition in leadership. Companies are no different. One of the most significant transitions in the Bible is when God transferred authority from Moses to Joshua just before Israel crossed the flooded Jordan River and entered the Promised Land.

Moses was a spiritual leader, and Joshua was his protégé and a tactical warrior well-equipped to help the people drive their enemies out of the Promised Land. The Lord's main command to Joshua was the following: *"This book of the Law shall not depart from your mouth, but you shall meditate on it day and night, so that you may be careful to do according to all that is written in it. For then you will make your way prosperous, and then you will have good success."* (Joshua 1:8 ESV).

At the close of 2020, I went through a transition in our business, handing over the president's role to my chief operating officer, BJ

Tarver. BJ was the first person I ever shared the Gospel with as we drove to work and crossed that Ship Channel Bridge in Houston, Texas, many years before. God moved BJ's heart on that vision trip to Colombia in 2012, and he has been growing in his faith ever since. It has been a joy to see the personal, professional, and spiritual growth of BJ and the rest of our team over the years. I am confident in their abilities and believe the company will move positively forward with the support of such an amazing team of people.

Between 2012 and 2020, my role focused much on moving Gulf Winds from a founder-led organization to a mission-led organization. Thanks to our incredible team members and leaders, our faith-based mission, values, foundation, and focus on people are now well-established. I hired a chief financial officer, Dustin Hebrank, and with his help, we provided increased financial transparency to our entire team, which has helped us better manage costs and focus on improving operating ratios. Together, we were able to achieve one of our goals, being named one of Houston's best places to work in 2018 by the *Houston Chronicle*—and in 2021, Energage named us a Top Workplace in the United States! We also expanded our transportation terminal footprint outside of Texas for the first time, establishing bases in Mobile, Alabama, and Memphis, Tennessee, with the goal of diversifying risk and expanding our mission. We are well-positioned for growth in the coming years, and it will be exciting to see our mission continue to expand.

Making the decision to officially hand the reins to someone else is not easy, even when you know it is the right thing to do. I had been considering a change for some time, but it was critically important to me that any move I made would benefit the whole company and align with our mission. While we absolutely care about corporate success, our team understands that we are not willing to sacrifice our mission and excellent workplace in the process. We know that people and profits must go together to succeed in living out our values and mission to

Delivering Hope

glorify God. Ultimately, where there is no margin, there is no mission. In addition, if there is no mission, the best margins are worthless.

Over the years, we discovered through trial and error that the tendency for most is to focus on people or profits, but the reality is that God cares deeply about both. Finding the appropriate balance can be very challenging, but it's worth the struggle to ensure that internal and external missional opportunities are maximized for the glory of God! The world seems to place maximum value on profits at the expense of people, or conversely, a cultural focus may take priority, and profits are squeezed out. As a mission-driven company, we must embrace the tension of valuing both, to the glory of God! If our motives are pure, we can absolutely strive for this goal daily and enjoy the journey to the fullest.

As leaders, the best way to balance this healthy tension is to set up the team for success. If that requires us to take on another role in the process, we need to do that to help the team move forward. In December 2020, I decided to

> *Where there is no margin, there is no mission.*

transition from president of Gulf Winds to chairman. The awesome part is that I now have more time to focus on growing the foundation and C12, which ultimately will result in an exponential Kingdom impact beyond Gulf Winds. In addition, BJ is fulfilling his calling, and our team gets a gifted and laser-focused leader, well-equipped for this next season of our growth and expansion. We are confident that our best days are ahead, and our Kingdom impact will be multiplied with these changes! Transitions are a part of life and, if embraced, can bring a lot of energy to any organization.

After Moses died, you can imagine the immense pressure Joshua must have felt as he was handed the task of leading the Israelites into the Promised Land. Moses had been their leader for decades and had faithfully brought them out from under the yoke of slavery in Egypt by the power of God. Most importantly, Moses had led Israel through a forty-year desert season that prepared the hearts of God's people to follow Him, to trust in His power, provision, and promises. Everyone loves times of harvest, but the real work and opportunity for growth come in times of planting and fertilizing. One generation was lost in the wilderness due to their idolatry and lack of obedience, but the next generation learned a great deal from the mistakes of their parents, and they were properly prepared to enter the Promised Land when the time came. Moses led the nation right up to the doorstep of the Promised Land, only to hand the baton off to Joshua.

God was very reassuring to Joshua during that process. He gave him specific instructions on how to lead and maintain His favor as he approached the monumental task of crossing the Jordan River and driving the Israelites' enemies out of the land.

> *No man shall be able to stand before you all the days of your life. Just as I was with Moses, so I will be with you. I will not leave you or forsake you. Be strong and courageous, for you shall cause this people to inherit the land that I swore to their fathers to give them. Only be strong and very courageous, being careful to do according to all the law that Moses my servant commanded you. Do not turn from it to the right hand or to the left, that you may have good success wherever you go. This Book of the Law shall not depart from your mouth, but you shall meditate on it day and night, so that you may be careful to do according to all that is written in it. For then you will make your way prosperous, and then you will have good success. Have I not commanded you? Be strong and courageous. Do not be frightened, and do not be dismayed, for the Lord your God is with you wherever you go.* (Joshua 1:5–9 ESV)

Notice the emphasis on doing things God's way. In a world that is full of self-help books, the Bible stands alone as the clear, living instruction manual for Christian leaders. In order to lead according to

Delivering Hope

God's ways, we must continually seek His counsel, overcome our fears, and rest in His good instruction.

God's Word: in our hearts and our corporate office! (Gulf Winds, 2020)

"All Scripture is breathed out by God and profitable for teaching, for reproof, for correction, and for training in righteousness, that the man of God may be complete, equipped for every good work."
—2 Timothy 3:16–17 (ESV)

This is my desire for Gulf Winds, our leadership team, and our foundation. I want God's best. I recognize that some readers will find this incredibly challenging, but as I have outlined in this book, God has led our company through so many ups and downs, and I have seen Him work so many miracles in the lives of people, that honestly, it would be harder for me to reject God at this point than to follow Him by faith in obedience.

Todd Stewart

Patrick Maher, me, BJ Tarver, and Dustin Hebrank (left to right) at the Steve Stewart Memorial Golf Tournament, 2017

Some of the Gulf Winds team at the Steve Stewart Memorial Golf Tournament, 2017

Delivering Hope

"And without faith it is impossible to please him, for whoever would draw near to God must believe that he exists and that he rewards those who seek him."
—Hebrews 11:6 (ESV)

Questions to Consider

1. What transitions are you facing in life?
2. How can Joshua 1:8–9 encourage you in this season of transition?
3. How does my story of handing over the reins of Gulf Winds challenge and encourage you to move forward with a transition in your life?

Chapter 15
The Good News!

"You didn't think, did you, that just by pointing your finger at others you would distract God from seeing all your misdoings and from coming down on you hard? Or did you think that because he's such a nice God, he'd let you off the hook? Better think this one through from the beginning. God is kind, but he's not soft. In kindness he takes us firmly by the hand and leads us into a radical life-change."
—Romans 2:3–4 (MSG)

Chances are that if you are still reading this book, you have a desire to follow God's will for your life, and you want to use your business or vocation to reach people with the Good News of Jesus Christ. On the other hand, maybe you are still a doubter. If so, I have another great story for you!

God Interrupts a Free Trip to Costa Rica

This one is about a man who decided to take a free ICM vision trip to Costa Rica in 2019. I was working around the house on a Sunday afternoon when I received a call from my son, Lane, who was on that trip. He said, "Dad, I have someone who wants to talk with you."

I said, "Great! Put them on."

The gentleman who got on the phone spoke in a quivering voice, as if he had just witnessed something that was impossible to explain. He cried as he told me that he was the husband of one of our employees and that I needed to know his story. Apparently, this couple had been at odds for a long time. Basically, the guy told me that he was only in Costa Rica for the free trip, and his intention was to separate from his family after the vacation. But God had other plans!

Mike and Tonya on our vision trip to Costa Rica

Mike sharing the testimony of how God transformed his life on that trip!

Delivering Hope

After visiting a few churches and hearing life-changing testimonies of how people were saved from sin, addiction, and shame through Jesus Christ, this gentleman decided that God was speaking to him directly. Shortly thereafter, the congregants at the church where they were worshiping surrounded him and prayed over him. He wept as he told me how he had never experienced that kind of love before. God set him free from a lot of baggage that he had been carrying for many years because of his challenging childhood and the things he had seen and done in his life. Major destructive addictions were broken in that instant. His marriage was restored on the spot, and this man is now growing in the Lord and serving in his local church.

I don't know what is in your heart today, but I want you to know that God loves you and He is still in the miracle business. How amazing that God has a plan for our lives and that He desires to have a relationship with each of us, no matter what we have done in the past. Truly, this is such Good News!

For God So Loved the World

> *"For God so loved the world that he gave his only Son, that whoever believes in him should not perish but have eternal life. For God did not send his Son into the world to condemn the world, but in order that the world might be saved through him."*
> —John 3:16–17 (ESV)

You do not have to live under condemnation and sin. You can live a full life in the Spirit that honors God, no matter what is in your past. The Bible tells us that we all fall short of God's holy standard. We are all in the same boat!

> *"For all have sinned and fall short of the glory of God."*
> —Romans 3:23 (ESV)

That said, we can live a *full* life with God's help!

> *"There is therefore now no condemnation for those who are in Christ Jesus. For the law of the Spirit of life has set you free in Christ Jesus from the law of sin and death."*
> —Romans 8:1–2 (ESV)

We do have to receive the gift of mercy and grace that God offers through His Son, Jesus Christ, in order to have a relationship with Him. We cannot earn salvation on our own through good works or just being a good person. It is a gift from God that we do not deserve, and which we must receive from Him by faith.

> *"For by grace you have been saved through faith. And this is not your own doing; it is the gift of God, not a result of works, so that no one may boast."*
> —Ephesians 2:8–9 (ESV)

This gift brings us an eternal peace that cannot be explained!

> *"Be anxious for nothing, but in everything by prayer and supplication, with thanksgiving, let your requests be made known to God; and the peace of God, which surpasses all understanding, will guard your hearts and minds through Christ Jesus."*
> —Philippians 4:6–7 (ESV)

God's offer is for everyone!

> *"For everyone who calls on the name of the Lord will be saved."*
> —Romans 10:13 (ESV)

Delivering Hope

Would you trust in Jesus Christ today by faith?

"Because, if you confess with your mouth that Jesus is Lord and believe in your heart that God raised him from the dead, you will be saved."
—Romans 10:9 (ESV)

Questions to Consider

1. How has God interrupted your life?
2. What do you think God is trying to communicate to you through this chapter?
3. Would you trust Jesus Christ by faith today?

Invitation

If you desire to trust Jesus by faith today, you can pray a simple prayer like the one below.

God in Heaven, I know that You love me beyond anything I could possibly even imagine. I also know that I am a sinner in need of Your amazing grace and mercy. Today, Lord, I repent of my sins—past, present, and future—and trust Jesus Christ by faith. I know that Jesus died for my sins, was buried in a tomb, and rose from the grave three days later. I know that Jesus took on the punishment that I deserve. Today, I am proclaiming that Jesus Christ is my Lord and Savior. Please fill me with the Holy Spirit, Lord, and help me to walk in your ways all the days of my life. Thank You, Lord Jesus, for loving me and for shedding Your precious blood for me. Help me to be the person that You want me to be from this day forward. Amen.

I hope this book has encouraged you to use your life and business for the glory of God. Truly, there is no greater joy than to walk in the good works that God has prepared for those who love Him (Ephesians 2:10).

Desire that your life count for something great! Long for your life to have eternal significance. Want this! Don't coast through life without a passion.[7]
—John Piper, Don't Waste Your Life

If sinners be damned, at least let them leap to Hell over our bodies. If they will perish, let them perish with our arms about their knees. Let no one go there unwarned and unprayed for.[8]
—Charles Spurgeon

---

[7] John Piper, *Don't Waste Your Life* (Crossway, 2003), 46.
[8] Charles Spurgeon, quoted in Greg Morse, "Over Our Dead Bodies: Embracing the Costs of Warning the Lost," *Desiring God*, January 19, 2018, https://www.desiringgod.org/articles/over-our-dead-bodies.

Chapter 16
Multiplying Ministry Through a Sale

"The point is this: whoever sows sparingly will also reap sparingly, and whoever sows bountifully will also reap bountifully. Each one must give as he has decided in his heart, not reluctantly or under compulsion, for God loves a cheerful giver. And God is able to make all grace abound to you, so that having all sufficiency in all things at all times, you may abound in every good work."
—2 Corinthians 9:6–8 (ESV)

"All businesses transition" is a phrase I heard many times over the years inside and outside of C12 circles. That said, and for all the reasons written in the previous chapters, I never dreamed I would actually sell Gulf Winds International. Aside from a few updates and this chapter, this whole book was written during COVID. Marketplace ministry was my calling at Gulf Winds, so the thought of a sale was truly never on my mind.

For many years, I ignored countless calls, texts, and emails about selling the business. If I did pick up the phone by accident, I would politely tell the potential buyers or their agents that Gulf Winds was a ministry, not for sale. After COVID and my personal leadership transition, that all changed. In hindsight, perhaps I saw it coming, but in the moment, it felt like a direct download from God.

In the early spring of 2022, I was sitting in the parking lot of United City Church in Humble, TX, getting updates on the business from leadership, when I just knew it was time. Many factors came together at that point, which made the decision super clear to me.

First, my personal transition impacted the decision, as I was no longer directly involved in the business except for minor leadership oversight. While confident in our leadership change, the ministry side of Gulf Winds had also been handed off; it was easier for me to consider a sale knowing other leaders were in place, and my time of direct influence as a steward had passed.

Second, COVID had created a lot of unique business opportunities in the global logistics space. Our company and team made some great business decisions to take full advantage of the positive freight environment, resulting in ever-increasing opportunities and profits. The post-COVID marketplace offered a homerun for our business. The team was executing at a high level, and we were also in the best cash position we had been in for many years. Our leadership team remained diligent and faithful to pay off debt from the first partner buyout, and we closed legacy facilities to focus on our core services. I knew the value of Gulf Winds was in an up cycle, and if we were going to sell, that would be the time. The thought of capitalizing on this opportunity seemed right for me personally, for my family, the nonprofit foundation ministry, as well as the team that had labored with us for so many years through the ups and downs. I knew deep down this was a rare opportunity. It would benefit many in ways that would take years to replicate.

Third and probably most notable, I truly believed for the first time in my working life that God could do more with the foundation and me outside the business than within. This was a *huge* revelation and comfort. I knew if the company's value was accurate, we could bless our people immensely as well as transition exponential money to fuel kingdom work.

I drove up to Hemphill, TX to meet my mother and let her know my decision. We sat on her back porch overlooking Toledo Bend reservoir, and she listened as I shared my heart.

View from Mom's house in Hemphill, Texas

To my delight, the news did not surprise her in the least. She confirmed the calling she and my father knew would come one day—to multiply my time and resources in ministry outside the four walls of the company—and she was actually excited for me and the team. I'm so thankful for my mother and father. Their willingness to risk it all later in life impacted so many lives, and they had extended faithful support to my leadership and direction of the company for so many years, including Mom's support for the potential sale of Gulf Winds.

Mom and I around the time of the Gulf Winds sale in 2022

So, I gave the go-ahead for our investment bankers to value the business. While it seemed strange to say those words, I had a profound peace about the decision.

I had been through this process ten years earlier, but this time, I would not be leading the team or creating the "marketing book," as in our first valuation process. In fact, I removed myself from all discussions and meetings with potential buyers with the exception of one, since I had no desire to stay on in any capacity. This was a very strange feeling as the owner of a multigenerational, family-owned business, one I had grown with from the time there was only one customer and one location. It would be like giving your son or daughter to someone you know and saying, "Go find a good home for the child." Nevertheless, I knew it was the right way to go about it; I needed to trust the process and the team. The buyers needed to buy the business and the team, not me.

Delivering Hope

The investment bankers confidently landed on a solid value range for the business based on their experience in the space, and we scheduled a time to meet. I prayed fervently before the meeting, listening to "Worthy of It All" by CeCe Winans on repeat in my truck as I drove to it. When I pulled up to the feeder road by the hotel, though, I drove right past. I needed more time to worship before walking into the meeting.

When we finally sat down, the bankers handed me and our executive leadership team a book that outlined the market and our proposed value, should we decide to move forward with finding a potential buyer. I asked everyone if I could pray in that moment, and I prayed that God would make it very clear if we were to sell Gulf Winds. I had a number in my head that I believed would be enough to bless our people and continue the ministry, but I wanted zero regrets. If they didn't offer enough, I felt perfectly fine shaking hands and continuing on as the business steward. Deep down, though, I knew it would be enough. God is a God of multiplication. He heard my cry, and when the bankers turned the page to the proposed value, it sat at exactly double what I had in my mind! *Thank you, Jesus!* I thought to myself.

> *God is a God of multiplication.*

Parable of the Talents

A wonderful parable in the Scriptures demonstrates the value of multiplication, and we experienced it firsthand.

> *"For it is just like a man about to go on a journey, who called his own slaves and entrusted his possessions to them. To one he gave five talents, to another, two, and to another, one, each according to his own ability; and he went on his journey. The one who had received*

the five talents immediately went and did business with them, and earned five more talents. In the same way the one who had received the two talents earned two more. But he who received the one talent went away and dug a hole in the ground, and hid his master's money.

"Now after a long time the master of those slaves came and settled accounts with them. The one who had received the five talents came up and brought five more talents, saying, 'Master, you entrusted five talents to me. See, I have earned five more talents.' His master said to him, 'Well done, good and faithful slave. You were faithful with a few things, I will put you in charge of many things; enter the joy of your master.'

"Also the one who had received the two talents came up and said, 'Master, you entrusted two talents to me. See, I have earned two more talents.' His master said to him, 'Well done, good and faithful slave. You were faithful with a few things, I will put you in charge of many things; enter the joy of your master.'

"Now the one who had received the one talent also came up and said, 'Master, I knew you to be a hard man, reaping where you did not sow, and gathering where you did not scatter seed. And I was afraid, so I went away and hid your talent in the ground. See, you still have what is yours.'

"But his master answered and said to him, 'You worthless, lazy slave! Did you know that I reap where I did not sow, and gather where I did not scatter seed? Then you ought to have put my money in the bank, and on my arrival I would have received my money back with interest. Therefore: take the talent away from him, and give it to the one who has the ten talents.'

Delivering Hope

"For to everyone who has, more shall be given, and he will have an abundance; but from the one who does not have, even what he does have shall be taken away. And throw the worthless slave into the outer darkness; in that place there will be weeping and gnashing of teeth." (Matthew 25:14–30 NASB)

In the coming months, the team ran through the gauntlet of potential buyer interviews, and we settled on a buyer. This process was long and arduous for all involved, not to mention the substantial business needs that do not disappear simply because you choose to sell.

Jamie Hampton, who manages our Hope Legacy Collective foundation, partnered with me to pray daily for the team by name and for the right buyer. We did not miss a day, and God truly honored and answered many prayers throughout the process. I selected a buyer after detailed input from our executive leadership team and investment bankers. Then, I signed the paperwork on my mother's birthday: November 6, 2022. This is significant because my father's birthday is November 8, and some of his last words to me were, "Take care of your mom."

The process of a sale is difficult, given the countless financial and legal due diligence requests from all involved, but great support from a reputable investment banking firm that had done their homework and knew the industry helped streamline the work. They kept everyone moving toward a mutually beneficial goal. The process takes a toll on everyone for sure, but it can be a great blessing in the end.

Deciding how much to give away, then wrestling with the emotions and inevitably difficult discussions that money and transition bring out in people is gut-wrenching and exhilarating at the same time. When possible, I am a fan of in-person meetings for hard monetary conversations, given the significance and finality of a business sale. Something about shaking hands and looking into someone's eyes makes a real difference.

My testimony is that prayer, faith, and a heart of generosity can overcome all of these difficulties in transition seasons when our motives are pure. If this is all kept in perspective, along with a spirit of prayer, anything is possible.

In the last week of the sale process, with all the negotiations complete, we landed on a closing date. Yet the date arrived, and we did not close. As you can imagine, the whole team sat on pins and needles, ready to complete the process, and I certainly did as well. I opened my Bible that day—December 17, 2022—and it fell open to the following Old Testament passage.

> *"Do not fear, for I am with you;*
> *Do not be afraid, for I am your God.*
> *I will strengthen you, I will also help you,*
> *I will also uphold you with My righteous right hand."*
> **(Isaiah 41:10 NASB)**

The significance of this cannot be overstated. This verse is on my father's tombstone. In that moment, at the end of the whole process, it was like my Heavenly Father and earthly dad reached down out of heaven and said, "I got you, son!" I wrote, *"Thanks, Dad,"* in the margin of my Bible!

Cheerful Giving

The sale went through on a detailed Zoom call while Nikki and I sat in my truck in a parking lot in the Houston Heights area. Very soon afterward, God allowed us to fund the Hope Legacy Collective foundation and bless our people immensely! Moving the money into a foundation yielded wonderful tax savings and eliminated any potential temptation for the misuse of funds. For anyone considering a sale, many wonderful tax and giving strategies should be considered pre-sale.

Delivering Hope

Thanks go to my friends at Arkos Global Advisors for helping us consider our options and execute a sustainable giving strategy.

Sarah Fontenot, Jeff Thomas, Nikki, and I signing papers to fund the Hope Legacy Collective after selling Gulf Winds

We experienced so much joy in giving to others!

Todd Stewart

The Gulf Winds legacy continues under new ownership, and we continue to deliver hope through the Hope Legacy Collective year after year! By funding our foundation with the sale of our business and partnering with other Christian foundations, we have experienced exponential ministry impact in our city and around the world. Here is just one testimony from a family who received support, encouragement, and care from Hope Legacy while navigating the challenges of cancer:

> *I'm so thankful for our God and Savior's healing power, and the way He assembles people in our path who are destined to support us in time of need. I'm thankful for His use and purpose of Hope Legacy Collective and Gulf Winds! Gulf Winds may be a transportation and warehousing provider, but actually, that is just an avenue to connect with people and do God's work on earth. Such a blessing.*

Just recently, we joined with Core Group Resources, a C12 company, and a couple of other Christian foundations to fund the RISE Initiative. "RISE focuses on providing job placement and career support to the underemployed, vulnerable populations, and those with barriers to employment by partnering with employers in search of top-tier talent."[9] We have found that our ministry impact is multiplied when joining with other like-minded businesses, foundations, and nonprofits to meet needs in our city. We are better together!

Internationally, we have sought to use our gifts as matching funds for Christian nonprofit ministries that are doing great work. Most recently, we joined Groundwire and Mission X Mission on a collaborative effort to reach young people on social media with the Good News of Jesus Christ. Millions of young people are coming to Christ through digital evangelism, but funding the marketing efforts is paramount!

---

[9] "Core Group Cares Launches RISE Initiative To Support Job Prospects for Vulnerable Populations," *Katy Times*, August 2, 2024, https://katytimes.com/stories/core-group-cares-launches-rise-initiative-to-support-job-prospects-for-vulnerable-populations,82010#.

Delivering Hope

A sale can provide much-needed fuel to fund local and international ministry efforts for the good of our communities and the glory of God!

Gulf Winds is truly a God story that keeps on giving! I'm so thankful to each and every past, present, and future team member and nonprofit partner who plays a role in living out this incredible missional journey with us! My prayer is that by sharing portions of our story, God would encourage and multiply His incredible mercy and grace in the lives of many more in the marketplace, here and around the world, for generations to come!

Be Bold for Jesus!
Todd

Questions to Consider

1. What is your transition plan?
2. Have you considered the exponential ministry value of your business post-sale?
3. How has our story caused you to think differently about a potential sale of your business?

Therefore, since we have been justified by faith, we have peace with God through our Lord Jesus Christ. Through him we have also obtained access by faith into this grace in which we stand, and we rejoice[d] in hope of the glory of God. Not only that, but we rejoice in our sufferings, knowing that suffering produces endurance, and endurance produces character, and character produces hope, and hope does not put us to shame, because God's love has been poured into our hearts through the Holy Spirit who has been given to us.
—Romans 5:1-5 (ESV)

Acknowledgments

To Nikki, my wife and God-ordained helpmate in this life. No one knows or understands the innumerable challenges and pressures that I/we faced on this journey more than you. Your faithfulness and ability to provide me with valuable perspectives while taking care of our kids is a BIG part of our God story. Thank You for taking this wild *faith* journey with me! I Love You! The best is yet to come!

To Lane, our firstborn—you are the smartest person I know. You have a servant's heart and ability to quickly evaluate complex issues and obstacles while simultaneously offering viable solutions, in any environment. You read people very well and have a stubborn spirit, just like your mom! You are exponentially more capable and valuable than you often give yourself credit for. You are a big part of our story. God is using you to build His Kingdom! Challenge yourself, do the work, and trust God!!! You will make a wonderful husband and father. I love you and I am proud of you!!!

To Lexi, our daughter—you were born a vocal and visionary leader. When I look at you, I see a reflection of myself in so many ways. You are a wonderful sister, mother, wife, and daughter. You have the heart of a lion and the wounds to prove it. Thank you for allowing me to share parts of your story in our larger story to deliver hope to many who need it. Keep dreaming, speaking truth, and casting vision for the good of our family and God's glory! I love you and I am proud of you.

Todd Stewart

Landon, my son-in-law/third son, welcoming you to our family has been one of the most joyous seasons of our lives. We truly gained a son, and I am excited to see how God will continue to multiply His grace and mercy through you in all areas of your life. You are a capable and gifted communicator with a bright mind. You have a tender heart for people and I have no doubt that you will enhance our legacy of *faith* and establish one of your own to God's glory! I love you and I am proud of you as a father, husband, and son!

Wren, granddaughter, you are almost two years old and have already made a massive mark on our family. It is true that grandchildren bring exponential joy and blessings to our lives far beyond what we could have ever imagined! Pawpaw loves you so much and I hope as you read this book one day that you realize how BIG our God really is! My deepest prayer for you is that you would love God and serve Him with your whole being. I pray daily that you would trust Jesus from a young age and that God would use you to multiply the Gospel exponentially! I believe you will be a powerful voice for Jesus as you grow up to God's glory! Jesus loves you and I love you so so so MUCH!!!

Jamie, my second son, as I reflect on our faith journey over the last ten-plus years, I am constantly reminded of the value of a friend that sticks closer than a brother. It's been an honor and joy to be a part of your story and to watch you grow and thrive as a son, husband, and father. God has been faithful! I know that our prayers will continue to carry this message of *hope* forward by the grace of God. We get to do this!!!

Mom, none of this would be possible without your love and support. Thank you for your sacrifice and the faithful love that you showed to me and Dad over the life of your marriage. I am confident that many people will benefit from the hope that is found in our story!

To the many Gulf Winds team members, some of whom now have companies of their own, who are now dispersed across Houston and around the nation serving in the logistics field, thank you! Whether you

Delivering Hope

are currently a Gulf Winds team member or have moved on to pursue other career aspirations, I am thankful you chose to be part of our story, and I am rooting for you!

To my editors, Kristin and Karla—this finished work is a result of your faithful support. I'm praying God multiplies His grace and mercy in your lives as this story is read by many, to God's glory! Thank You!!!

THANK YOU FOR READING MY BOOK!

Download Your Free Gifts: Just to say thanks for buying and reading my book, I would like to give you a few free bonus gifts, no strings attached!

Scan the QR Code:

I appreciate your interest in my book and value your feedback, as it helps me improve future versions. Please leave your invaluable review on Amazon.com with your feedback. Thank you!

www.ingramcontent.com/pod-product-compliance
Lightning Source LLC
LaVergne TN
LVHW041337080426
835512LV00006B/504